The Full Catastrophe

The Full Catastrophe

TRACEY LEONARD

HiddenSpring

Designed by Bookhouse Digital, Sydney

A catalogue record for this book is available from the Library of Congress.

Library of Congress Control Number: 2010932161

ISBN: 978-1-58768-061-8

First published in the United States of America in 2010 by
HiddenSpring
An imprint of Paulist Press
997 Macarthur Boulevard
Mahwah, New Jersey 07430
United States of America

www.paulistpress.com

Printed and bound in the United States of America

For Sister Luke and my mother, Joan,
with thanks and love

Contents

PREFACE

Life is a series of changes. From birth to death we make and remake our lives, depending on where we live and the people involved with us at the time. We live with the fallacy that we can control our own destiny. The choices we make and the impulses acted on or not can change our lives irreversibly.

If not for the fickle hand of fate on 23 October 1988, I would not have written this book. Disasters are something that I coped with as a nurse in India and on Aboriginal settlements. I considered myself capable of handling any difficult situation.

My own personal disaster changed my life forever. Gone was my super-confident nurse persona with the can-do attitude. Replaced by a cerebral and reflective me. It is in this reflective state that I am now able to travel to all the hidden rooms of memory and selfishly dwell upon past experiences. It is with a deep sense of gratitude that I can now relive these events and know that most of my impulsive decisions only enriched my life.

I finally decided to share my memory travels with a computer screen. In the pages that follow I've tried to keep imagination under control because it's memory I want to tap. Fiction is often a pale reflection of reality and these stories give full force to the power of life.

T.L.

PART ONE

Assault on the Senses
Calcutta, May 1981–January 1982

 'Calcutta assaults the senses like no other city on earth' says the official government tourist brochure. Here I am seated in an aeroplane ready to approach Calcutta Airport when I read my first tourist information. Mild panic sets in as I try to contemplate the assault that awaits. Maybe this isn't such a good idea.

Having just qualified as a nurse in Toowoomba, Queensland, I am filled with the idealism of youth and the need for adventure. I heard the teeming millions crying out for me and now I'm in the air, circling Calcutta and having a panic attack. My family and friends told me I was mad. As this was not a new refrain, it made no impression.

I only made a definite decision to come to India three weeks ago, after my application to work at Darwin Hospital was rejected. I have always been somewhat impulsive and this is looking like one of my more foolhardy decisions. The only preparation I made for this trip was speaking with a fellow who worked as a volunteer here a few years ago. He gave me Mother Teresa's address and a general outline of Calcutta. But what I may lack in forward planning and preparation is more than compensated for by instinctive cunning, and I attach myself to the Australian guy beside me, a practical type of the travel guidebook and basic research school of thought. Mind you, Greg is looking as scared as I am and is grateful for the company.

*

Once outside the terminal, the heat and humidity wraps around us like an overcoat. According to our new bible, the best way into town is by bus. Finding the right one and getting a seat boosts our confidence immensely, but our new-found enthusiasm ebbs away as quickly as the sweat pouring from our bodies. There appears to be no bus driver. Patience is obviously the first of many lessons to be learnt on this journey.

Drowsing in my seat I am startled by a keening outside the window. As I watch, dozens of beggars swarm around the bus. Nothing could have prepared me for this first sight. Deformed and crippled bodies jostle with mothers carrying babies while all around them children scream 'baksheesh'. My hand stays guiltily in my pocket as this first brush with the teeming millions is dealt with by our tardy driver.

The drive into Calcutta resembles the build-up of a symphonic crescendo. Lush green foliage gives way to villages, then industrial complexes, followed by small businesses and markets which grow in density and height until there is not a single square metre of unoccupied space on either side of the road. This visual peak is ably supported in sound, to the extent of sensory overload. The assault has begun.

Our bus is trapped in a traffic jam. Buses, trams, cars, rickshaws, bullock carts and thousands of pedestrians vie for right of way. Horns, bells and voices compete mercilessly in some bizarre form of noise ritual. According to the map in the bible, we are reasonably close to our destination. Armed with desperation and perspiration, Greg and I descend into the throng.

Once on the sidewalk, I am relieved of my bag by a young Indian boy. He places it on his head and says firmly, 'Come, hotel.' We have no alternative but to follow my fast-disappearing bag. Twenty minutes later the bag halts outside a building. We assume this is a hotel, although no sign confirms this. I reclaim my bag as our young helper ventures inside. Raised and angry voices follow him back to the street. With a shrug of the shoulders he informs us, 'No room. Come.' This scenario recurs several more times before we arrive at the Timestar Hotel. At least this one has a sign.

The Timestar is a decrepit, three-storey building. Inhabitants of the lobby include four sleeping bodies, assorted dogs and several rodents. Amazingly, a room with a glowing description is available, a double room with electricity and water, price 30 rupees ($3). By this stage Greg and I are thankful just to have found something.

The manager leads us up two flights of steps, carefully stepping round a few more sleeping bodies. He unlocks the door and leaves us the key. The room itself is about three metres by two and a half, with two beds and bare mattresses. In the corner is a plastic bucket containing water. Greg tries the light and fan switches without success. The accumulation of the day's events so far are too much for me and I collapse weeping onto the bed. This emotional breakdown lasts only a few minutes before I realise the bed is alive and biting. A few quick strides across the room and I plunge my head into the water bucket. At least this is cool and slightly refreshing. Greg and I decide there must be something better out there and set out to find it.

Wandering around the streets, concentrating on avoiding the garbage and filth, pursued by children and other helpful Indians, we suddenly come upon a garish green wall and two large iron gates. The sign overhead proclaims the Fairlawn Hotel. Pushing through the gates is like entering the Garden of Eden. Tables and chairs are sheltered by umbrellas, and fairy lights are strung through the trees and lush garden. Uniformed waiters are serving ice-cold beer to several of the guests. Greg and I feel like characters in *The Wizard of Oz.*

Waiting at the desk to greet us is Mrs Vi Smith, owner, hostess and Queen of the Fairlawn. Mrs Smith is like a carefully preserved relic of the British Raj. Her face is meticulously made up, with high arching eyebrows, bright green eye shadow, long dark eyelashes and a strategically placed beauty spot above her lip. Carefully coiffured hair manages to stay sculptured even in the humidity. Her dress is Western and somewhat suggestive of the style of Elizabeth II. The lobby area is like a shrine to the British royal family. Photographs of the Queen, Prince Philip and Prince

Charles adorn the walls. I am left in no doubt as to where Mrs Smith's loyalties lie.

Greg and I approach with some trepidation and enquire about the price of a room. Sensing the need in Mrs Smith for a little drama, I tell her the story of our day so far. When I reach the part about the Timestar, she says, 'I hope you didn't leave your bags there, did you?' At this point she tells us we could have a room for 150 rupees (A$15). We gratefully accept and make haste back to the Timestar.

We creep as quietly as we can over the bodies and various animals until we reach our room. To our great surprise and relief our bags are still here, unmolested. We grab them and make a cautious exit via the back stairs. I feel no pang of conscience for failing to pay for the room.

Back in the safe and reassuring confines of the Fairlawn, Mrs Smith shows us our room. It is only a single with another bed brought in. Besides clean sheets and pleasant if somewhat fussy decor, its distinctive feature is a shower with hot and cold water. I claim first use and start to regain some equilibrium after scrubbing from head to toe. Refreshed and cool again, Greg and I discuss our day so far. Each acting out of a sense of bravado, we manage to find the humour in the situation and give each other the courage to go on. Greg's plan is to travel around India for the next three months. My somewhat hazy plan is to work for Mother Teresa here in Calcutta. Tonight is a breathing space: tomorrow we will have to learn to live in this country.

 By the second day Greg and I have quizzed everyone we've met at the hotel about Calcutta and about India in general. We are ready to pass through the gates and face reality.

Sudder Street plays host to varied tenants. From the Chowringhee end, the Indian Museum takes up one whole block. This is bordered by a large and potentially ankle-breaking rats' warren, with accompanying garbage dump. The putrid stench acts as an effective quasi-warning system. Footpath travel appears almost impossible. A few metres on from the rats, small clusters of people begin to appear. Each group comprises an entire family unit. Here are my teeming millions and it strikes me as quite ironic that they are far better equipped to deal with this city than I am. They are living their lives here on the pavement. Cooking fires burn a pungent concoction of cow dung and coal dust. Children laugh and play in the run-off around the water pump. They are quick to size us up, grab our hands and beg for money. Seasoned but as yet not hardened campaigners, they soon lose interest.

Moving further down the street, the Salvation Army hostel is adjacent to the Fairlawn. Hopefully I will find cheap and clean accommodation here later. Forward progress is erratic. Clad only in a basic pair of thongs, I am starting to have neck spasms from looking ahead and down with each step. So far I have trodden in every form of human and animal waste and stubbed my toes against numerous empty green coconut shells. The rest of the street boasts small restaurants and many tiny cubbyholes which pass for shops. There are a few buildings where people live and a couple more hotels.

Having survived one whole street, we enter a cafe for a cup of tea. Two teas are served in glasses containing what passes for milk and about two table-spoons of sugar. Obviously at some stage we must learn the art of ordering in a way that gets you what you want. Greg and I have a new and improved Calcutta street map and while he is happy to explore the city, I feel that I should make contact with Mother Teresa's organisation. The only information I have is an address: 54a Lower Circular Road. As we study the map it dawns on us that a lot of names have been changed since the map was printed. The street that houses the US consulate has been changed to Ho Chi Minh Sarani. This perverse display of humour makes me feel right at home. Unfortunately many other street names have gone the same way. It's like a who's who of past communist leaders. Lower Circular Road could be the reincarnation of any of them. We decide to leave venturing down to Mother Teresa's until after lunch.

Back at the Fairlawn, Mrs Smith interprets the map for us and we head out again. The route looks simple enough. Down Sudder Street, right into Free School Street, the first street on the left, follow it straight along until we come to a main road and this should be Lower Circular Road. As we leave Free School Street, there is a progressive change in the environment. Ripon Street transforms from brick stucco buildings to a more narrow, congested, frantic commercial area. Once over the first intersection each small shop constitutes a hub of activity. Every form of mechanical repair is being carried out in the street, on the footpath or in little sheds. Interspersed with the many and varied engineering enterprises are paper and metal recyclers, tea shops and eating houses. They don't have far to go for their meat, as every fourth building is an open butcher shop. A man sits on a raised platform, surrounded by his knives and cleavers ready to serve his customers. All his produce hangs from hooks attached to a rail above his head. Blood and entrails mix with the rest of the gutter refuse to produce a heady and nauseating aroma, exacerbated by the baking heat. My feet are once again in the thick of it, while my eyes and nose threaten a flood. It is difficult to drag my eyes away as they register that each carcass has its tail left unskinned so that its origin may be discerned. Greg and I spend countless minutes trying to match the tail to the animal. They are definitely not cows, sheep or pigs. The dogs circling the area prove possible candidates, but I can't bear to pursue this train of enquiry. Maybe some things are better unknown.

Ripon Street continues to narrow and wind its way until the noise and sight of several lanes of traffic reveal Lower Circular Road. Fifty metres to the left stands a three-storey grey building with brown window shutters. A plaque reads, '54a Lower Circular Road, Missionaries of Charity'. Walking down the small lane-way we find a door and a long chain with a handle. Underneath, the sign says 'pull'. I follow the instructions and the door is opened by a sister in a blue-bordered sari. Success at last!

Inside is a half-open courtyard, with cement floor and cement benches on all three sides. A door at the far end opens into another courtyard. I explain to the sister my desire to work here in Calcutta. She tells us to wait and that someone will come. Greg and I take up positions and peer about the place like gawking tourists, which is exactly what we are, I suppose. I don't know what I expect to happen—Mother Teresa to come waltzing in and thank me for coming? To see some sign that a saint lives here? Some outward sign of holiness? My imagination soars on heroic and grand fantasies. Unfortunately the mundane business of real life drags me back.

There are several other people waiting, all of them Indian. The sisters deal with each of these in rapid fire Bengali with wild hand gestures. While watching all these goings-on my eyes continue to rake the upper balconies, hoping to catch sight of Mother Teresa. I'm like a groupie outside a rock star's hotel and it makes me sick. I had no idea that I would feel this way. The time drags on and after two hours of waiting the hero worship has turned to a 'bugger them, I'm going home' type of feeling.

Finally a white woman in a blue-bordered sari walks through the door and introduces herself as Sister Henrietta. As fate will have it, she is also Australian. After some ritual talk about home she gets down to business. She tells me about the various homes that they operate. There is Shishu Bhavan which is an orphanage; Prem Dan is a large home for the physically and mentally handicapped; Kalighat is the home for the dying and destitute; and Titigar is a leprosarium outside Calcutta. As well as the large homes there are numerous dispensaries, schools and other projects.

Sister Henrietta is far from welcoming me with open arms. A lot of volunteers come to Calcutta and it seems they can be more trouble than they are worth. She doesn't express it in these words exactly, but I catch the general meaning. Other basic information includes the fact that volunteers are expected to provide their own accommodation, meals and transport. She recommends either the Salvation Army or the YWCA. Rising to leave she suggests that I be here tomorrow at 8.00 a.m. to go with the sisters to the dispensary at Sealdah railway station. My heroic visions are well and truly shattered by now. There will be no grand acclaim or professions of gratitude for yet one more volunteer come to save the world.

 I wake early, with my stomach already churning. This is my third day in Calcutta and I wonder if I will ever feel comfortable here. The last two nights in the Fairlawn have provided a bulwark against the outside world, but today I must move out and find somewhere cheaper. I dress in jeans, T-shirt and thongs and make my way downstairs. After a quick cup of tea, Greg wishes me luck and with one last deep breath I am out of the gates.

I arrive at the Mother House without mishap, which lifts my spirits. Sister Henrietta points me in the direction of two young sisters. 'Come,' they instruct me, in what I soon learn is the standard Indian manner. I meekly obey and follow them out the door. Whatever thoughts I had of learning more about the dispensary are quickly dispelled when the sisters start reciting the rosary. Although I am a Catholic it has been many years since I have done the rounds of the rosary beads.

My two companions are both no more than seventeen and would be stretching to reach 150 centimetres. My height of 170 centimetres and well-muscled frame make me feel like a giant. Our little threesome attracts many comments and much hilarity.

I keep my head down and play follow the leader. Even travelling by tram, it is more than a five-decade of the rosary trip to Sealdah.

According to the travel guide, Sealdah railway station is the most densely populated area on earth at 9.00 a.m. each day. Thousands of people stream out of the exits, mingling with the resident platform population. Hawkers and sellers of every description merge with this mobile mass, trying to make a sale. Watching from the relative safety of my tram, the scene resembles a human tidal wave. My flickering enthusiasm is on the wane again. Following my two guides through the melee, I emerge onto a street with a low-set, red-brick building. 'Here,' one of the sisters announces. They obviously believe in an economical use of the English language.

Inside the middle building are three rooms. The first acts as a waiting room and storage area. The second consists of two wooden benches and two tables containing instruments and dressing material. In the middle of the room are four garbage bins, which in a previous life were large, square biscuit drums. The third room is the medication dispensary area, with a well-stocked pharmacy. The sister in charge calls everyone to attention and we all move into the first room. Here candles have been lit on a small altar. The sisters recite a prayer and sing a hymn and then it is all hands on deck.

A few other volunteers have turned up and are busily preparing the second room for the patients. I manage a feeble hello and stand against the wall to observe. The front window section of each red building is only steel mesh and allows a view both ways. The mass of people I thought were in transit are actually waiting to be attended to. The ceiling in the room is only about two and a half metres high and is covered with brown hessian. With no artificial light available, the open screen becomes imperative. Five volunteers and three sisters are attending to the patients as they come in. A man at the door regulates the flow, with anything but a caring attitude. The noise level grows with each minute, the heat and humidity keeping pace. By 9.15 a.m. babies and children are whimpering, crying and screaming. Patients and volunteers are shouting at each other in the mistaken belief that volume will translate French, German, English and Bengali into one decipherable language, although a surprising degree of success with this system can be seen as happy customers exit the building. Those on the outside looking in feel obliged to offer their opinions and diagnoses, as well as pleading the urgency of their particular case. The sweat is pouring from me as I stay glued to my wall. The solid brick room is only three and a half metres square and with five volunteers, three sisters and about eighteen patients, the high temperature and lack of air are stifling. The stench of decay and unwashed bodies mingles with the urine and diarrhoea odours of the babies. The dirty and diseased dressings removed from wounds mix with the blood, pus and other detritus gathering in the garbage bins.

From the relative safety of my wall, I quickly realise that the patients I had seen on the wards of St Vincent's in Toowoomba were a poor preparation for what I see before me now. No training on earth can prepare you for the sight of a baby with huge eyes sunken into its head, skin pulled tight across its face, a mouth too tired for sound, eyes too dry for tears. Matchstick arms and legs lie listless as the swollen abdomen almost consumes the child. But it's the eyes you can never forget; large, dark spheres hold your attention and silently plead for help. I have never felt so useless in my life.

One of the volunteers accompanies a mother and child to the local hospital, hoping for admission. As the endless crowd of people continues to flow through the door, one of the sisters directs some my way. Crouched down on the floor, I soon discover that my patient has come to have a dressing changed. Having observed several of these already, I feel confident enough to start. It is a leg ulcer and after cleaning it with disinfectant I ask a sister what to put on it. She directs me to the dressing table and says, 'That.' There is a choice: red for mercurochrome, purple for gentian violet, yellow for acriflavine and several tubes of ointment which are mostly of French origin with labels I can't understand. I opt for the good old standby of mercurochrome and bandage up the leg. My patient thanks me profusely and leaves. I treat a few more simple cases, keeping to the same colour scheme.

By 11.30 the patients have dwindled and clean-up begins. One of the Dutch volunteers, Weil, explains the workings of the dispensary and shows me where everything is stored. She has been working here for the last three weeks and seems to be enjoying it.

Contact with the sisters is very limited, to say the least. I go with the other volunteers for a cup of tea and am amused to see that four out of six of us reach for our cigarettes the moment we sit down. A universal stress reliever. Weil is several years older than me and is much more confident in her outlook. I have found a mentor to help me through the initial hurdles. As we walk back to Sudder Street she gives me the benefit of her three weeks of wisdom. I can only hope for such quick progress myself.

At the Salvation Army hostel I obtain a bed in a six-bed dormitory. It is pretty clean and I am given one clean sheet and pillowcase. The mattress even looks uninhabited. There is an attached bathroom with a cold shower and toilet. All this is mine for the princely sum of 10 rupees a day. All I have to do now is collect my things from the Fairlawn and begin this new phase in my journey.

 Over the next few days I go to the dispensary each morning. With Weil's guidance and my own observations I slowly learn to distinguish different conditions. Babies and children are regular customers, and besides chronic malnutrition—or because of it—they suffer numerous skin infections. Scabies and lice infect their bodies in an everlasting cycle. No amount of creams and lotions can disinfect the platform where they sleep, replenish their meagre possessions or ward off the rats, cats and dogs that burrow through their limited living space. What amazes me is how cheerful and alive these people are. With my Western eyes and limited knowledge, I pity them and wring my hands in frustration.

On one of these mornings I am drifting off into a save-the-world reverie when I am dragged back to reality by a grasping hand pulling me out the door. Here I am confronted by a woman whose hair is so matted and unkempt that it appears to have been plastered on. One glance at this mess is enough to tell me that thousands of tiny animals are now calling this head home. No-one will let the woman inside, so her hair will have to be removed out here in the gutter.

Judging by the total lethargy of the woman, she is far past caring. If I could get out of doing this and still retain some self-respect, I would. Unfortunately everyone else seems to be suddenly very busy. With an old pair of scissors and a futile attempt to find some gloves, I'm ready for action. Hairdressing has never been my forte. I make several cuts through the hair, stopping every few minutes to turn and breathe, such is the overpowering stench uncovered with each stroke. Large nits and other insects of all varieties come crawling out with each clump of hair removed. A large and vocal crowd has gathered for this sideshow, and my anger grows as I feel the woman beneath my hands tremble. Within twenty minutes I have removed most of her hair and have put a match to it in celebration. To my surprise and delight the woman revealed is both beautiful and grateful. I give her some lice shampoo and soap as she kisses my hands and expresses her thanks. I feel both humble and useful for the first time (though I also have feelings of guilt for not wanting to treat her and for being repulsed by the sight of her). My period of elation and accomplishment lasts for some time, after which I find myself eager to return to the Salvation Army hostel for a shower and shampoo. I scratch myself all the way there.

*

I am trying to establish some routine to my days. Each morning I go to Sealdah and work there until midday, with the afternoons spent reconnoitring the area around Sudder Street and beyond. Food is my biggest problem so far. My limited dietary preferences are sorely tested here. I have always been a fussy eater, and have managed to make it this far in life without eating most vegetables, eggs or dairy products. I am quickly coming to realise that my mother and many others were trying to improve my diet and not just inflict pain for their own pleasure all these years. I am equipped with a jar of Vegemite, and India has passable sliced bread on which I am surviving so far. This is yet another instance where I should have endeavoured to do at least a little research before embarking on this journey. It is ironic that I spend so much of my time thinking and dreaming about food, when all around me are the poor, hungry and homeless.

It is with a view to improving our living conditions that Weil and I move to the YWCA. This is situated in Middleton Row, only a few blocks from Sudder Street but a world away in aesthetic appeal. Middleton Row is just off Park Street and it is here that the more up-market restaurants, night clubs and shops are situated. The YWCA is a three-storey, green, brick and stucco building constructed in a 'U' shape. In the middle of the U are two clay tennis courts. Each storey has a balcony which looks out over the courts. A twin-share room here will cost us 30 rupees a day. Mrs Moffat is the person in charge and seems undecided on whether to welcome our custom or refuse us entry. She stresses repeatedly what a quiet and respectable establishment she runs and lays down a sheet of rules that guests must abide by. Eventually the payment of a week in advance and our assurances that we are of good character get us in.

The whole atmosphere at the YWCA is like a breath of fresh air for me. It makes me feel more stable and secure. Three meals a day are included in the price. Breakfast consists of toast, egg (fried, boiled or omelette), a banana and tea or coffee. Lunch is of the Indian variety—rice plus a variety of curries. Dinner is something of a mystery as the cook does his very quirky interpretation of Western cuisine. At least I can work my way through each of these meals and find enough of substance to keep me going. I may even be tempted into extending my very limited taste repertoire.

Another absolute bonus with the Y is the availability of hot water. Each wing has its own shower and toilet block and in the evening there are supposed to be hot showers. As with all things in Calcutta, what is meant to happen and what actually happens don't always correspond. Power blackouts seem to occupy twelve out of every twenty-four hours. I don't think that the power to every part of Calcutta is ever on at any one time. They have elevated the process of load-shedding into an art form. The water situation follows the same basic principle, namely: whenever you want it, it has just gone off. But it is so enticing to know that it could be working that you never totally lose heart. After all, surely it is worth waiting until midnight for one hot shower.

There are several other Mother Teresa volunteers living here, and a loose camaraderie develops between us. People come from many different countries: England, France, Germany, Canada and the United States. The diversity of backgrounds surprises me.

There are students, a secretary, a physiotherapist and teachers. They all work in different areas: two at the orphanage, some at Prem Dan and others at the home for the dying. One girl spends her day teaching the young sisters English. While most of the girls are Catholic, religion doesn't seem to be a major factor in why they came here. I have been down to the Mother House for mass, and while it is inspiring to see hundreds of sisters in devout prayer and marvel at the sparseness and simplicity of their lives, the mere thought of rising every morning at 5.15 a.m. is too much for me. I have never understood the religious fervour associated with dawn activities. If God never sleeps then he doesn't have to get up either. I don't function properly until after breakfast. Fortunately there are absolutely no rules about working here, which in itself is a strange experience.

 I have survived three weeks in Calcutta and now I am going out to Kalighat, the home for the dying and destitute. It is situated about 20 to 30 minutes bus ride from Park Street. Chowringhee is the main road in Calcutta and spreads across several lanes of traffic. Its convergence with Park Street provides a natural bus stop as the traffic has to slow to a standstill to accommodate the number of automobiles. There are no discernible transport or traffic regulations. The afternoons around 3.00 p.m. to 5.00 p.m. are the busiest time of the day. As each overcrowded, listing bus approaches my stop, I wonder how I will ever get to Kalighat. According to Weil we need a No. 76. A red double-decker almost topples over rounding the corner and thunders to a stop, scattering the few hundred of us waiting for a bus. The idea of returning to the YWCA seems very appealing. I cannot get used to the huge numbers of people always around me. Calcutta is a city of nine million and it feels like they are all out on the streets all the time. The constant jostling and manoeuvring is physically draining, and paranoia about pick-pockets and the ever-grasping arms of the beggars add to the mental fatigue.

At last a No. 76 arrives and with the help of many eager hands we are pushed and pulled inside. I have often wondered about the 'black hole of Calcutta' and now believe I have found it. There are bench seats along the sides of the bus and squashed between them are human sardines, vertically stacked. My left arm grips my bag with white-knuckled intensity while my right grips an overhead bar for support. We are packed in so tightly that the mass of people holds us upright, despite the lurching, stop–start style of driving. As a novice bus traveller I am unaware of the etiquette. Having been repeatedly fondled and groped about the breasts and buttocks, I resort to the elementary defence of elbows, knees and loud, foul expletives. This behaviour works extremely well and even provides a measure of distance around me. Weil has displayed her hard-won experience and lodged herself in the 'ladies only' section. Every little bit of knowledge contributes to survival. It is the longest twenty minutes of my life. Exiting the bus is a major undertaking, a bit like taking a blind step off a cliff. Having pushed your way to the door, one last surge of energy is needed to launch yourself into the outside world.

Kalighat Road is a very congested, narrow thoroughfare. The main businesses lining the street are shops selling saris and other clothing. Numerous stalls sell all sorts of paraphernalia for the goddess Kali. She is the goddess of death and represents the supreme night which swallows all that exists. Perhaps appropriately, she is the patron deity of Calcutta. Kali is portrayed in painting and effigy as a black figure

Kalighat's unobtrusive doorway, nestled between stalls in one of Calcutta's
busiest streets, belies the life and death dramas that take place within

laughing hideously as she dances on the prostrate
body of the god Shiva, a raised sword in one of her
four hands and a severed head in another. Alongside
these grotesque images are numerous flower-sellers,

anxious to make a sale to the many pilgrims travelling towards the temple. In another of Calcutta's many ironies, the temple for the goddess Kali is right beside the home for the dying. As Kalighat Road opens up to the temple area, the large, domed building of the temple dominates the scene. Beside this impressive structure the bland, yellow–brown Kalighat building with its single storey barely rates inspection. Cluttered stalls attached to its outer walls further reduce its visual impact.

Three small steps lead to the doorway and just inside is a plaque: 'Nirmal Hriday, Home for the Dying and Destitute'. Two more paces bring me straight into the ward. The first thing that hits me is the smell. Death, decay and despair mix in a pungent cocktail that no amount of disinfectant can ever hope to mask. The cloying aroma of Kalighat is enough to make me gag. My wild imaginings of this place have built up a turbulent emotional storm within me. The unknown is usually more frightening than reality, but in this case reality is every bit as scary as my dreams.

Beside my feet, beneath a shrine to the Virgin Mary, lies a man on a narrow bed. I know that he is alive only because I see his chest rise and fall. His eyes are partially open and staring blankly. Every bone in the man's body seems to be trying to pierce through his skin. A shiver runs down my spine as the sight of him reminds me of footage I've seen of the victims in the Holocaust. Gross feelings of self-doubt and inadequacy assail me as the magnitude of the horror hits me.

The ward is set out in rows. The left and right sides are elevated about 70 centimetres above floor level and each side holds about fifteen beds. Beds also stretch down the middle area with a small aisle at the left-hand side. Access to the patients on the raised right-hand side is limited to the distance between each bed on the middle level. Several more beds are crammed into the remaining space at either end of this ward to bring the total bed capacity to fifty-one. The beds themselves are made of metal and are long and narrow. A plastic-covered mattress about five centimetres thick completes the basic makeup. All the beds are covered with a bright green sheet, and all the patients are colour-coordinated in green pants and white shirts. The beds themselves are only 13 centimetres above floor level and about 40 centimetres apart. Above each is a number.

This is the physical and clinical layout of the ward. Describing the people on these beds is the hard part.

The men range in age from twelve to sixty, although Weil informs me that the average age is around thirty. Admission to Kalighat can occur in several ways. The most constant admissions are those people picked up from the street by the Calcutta City Council. These people must be refused admission to any of the city hospitals in order to qualify for a bed here. One look at the cargo in the back of a council ambulance is usually enough reason to pass them on as a hopeless case. The sisters and brothers also bring in people they have found lying in the streets. Another way to gain admittance is for the person to get themselves to the front door and pray that there is a spare bed and that the sister in charge will consider them sick enough for admission.

Malnutrition is at the root of every disease seen at Kalighat. Tuberculosis is endemic and complications arising from this disease are a common cause of admission. Dysentery in all its many forms is another leading contender. Malaria and countless other fever-related conditions are plentiful. Intestinal parasites, viral infections and old-fashioned trauma account for several other diagnoses. Each patient has a cocktail of these complaints, with some more severe than others.

The female ward is set out exactly like the male side. Blue is the colour of choice here and all the women wear checked gowns. There are fifty-seven female beds and I don't know whether this is because of their greater longevity than men or just availability of space. All the beds are occupied and the women seem more robust than their male counterparts, although several are just skin and bone and obviously not long for this world.

The middle section of Kalighat comprises the water storage tanks, a wash area and the morgue. At the top of the male ward is the administration desk, a large table and two grey metal medication cupboards. Next to this area is a large stove and cooking place. The stove is of the brick and clay variety with a large chimney stretching through the roof. On the roof of Kalighat are four small dwellings which serve as homes for the Indian workers and their families. Their various jobs include laundry duties, carpentry, building and keeping watch over the place at night. The roof area is also used to dry the laundry. It offers a great view around the streets and temple precinct, while also providing a calm spot in which to have a smoke.

Probably the most important element in the make-up of Kalighat is Sister Luke, the sister in charge of the whole operation. Nurses from whatever background can easily identify Sister Luke as a fearsome charge sister, the type who will certainly shoot you down should you be foolish enough to poke your head up. As with most charge sisters, she has a voice which carries its blunt message to the person receiving it and to anyone else within a half-kilometre radius; the loudspeakers of the temple are no match in volume. Sister Luke has run Kalighat for the past ten years. She and another sister are the only professed, or blue-bordered, sisters here. All the others are young novices; this is their learning experience and part of their training. Sister Luke runs everything, from administration, diagnosis and treatment, stores and supplies, admissions and discharges to the workers' wages and family disputes. She barely tolerates volunteers and will only speak to you if you survive a couple of weeks and she has assessed you as genuine. Any volunteer stupid enough to waltz into Kalighat and give Sister Luke the benefit of their ideas is usually given an earful and told of the great spiritual benefits in emptying bedpans. Needless to say these types don't hang around for long.

On this first overwhelming day I'm more than happy to keep my head down, mouth shut and work quietly in the cleaning and feeding department. No special skills are required and the close contact with the individual patients removes the fear and intimidation

I had first felt. The basics of life never change, be they for rich or poor; everyone wants a clean bed and body and enough to eat and drink.

Language barriers exist between many different groups in India as there is no unifying language. Fourteen separate languages are recognised and hundreds of local dialects. Bengali is the language of Calcutta and is completely different from the language spoken by the sisters from Kerala. Eventually I find that a handful of Bengali words mixed with English, mime and eye movement will suffice. The afternoon shift finishes at 6.00 p.m. and it's back to the buses once more.

 I have been in Calcutta for six weeks now and have finally settled in. People say that if you can survive the first month you may even grow to love the place, but I doubt this will ever happen to me. My life at the YWCA has improved even further with the availability of a single room. Paid on a monthly basis, No. 18 is now all mine. Its walls only stretch three-quarters of the way to the ceiling, but the illusion of privacy is all that matters in this city of millions. My little haven consists of a bed, dressing-table, chair and a built-in wardrobe. There is also a large window that opens onto the apartment building next-door. A ceiling fan and light complete the list of amenities. This little oasis is enough to recharge me each evening.

Work has fallen into a pattern: Sealdah in the morning and Kalighat in the afternoon. I really enjoy the dispensary and am getting to recognise the regulars. It is almost like a family reunion each time they return. The kids have a wonderful sense of humour and quite often we end up in a water fight.

The weather is getting more humid with every passing day and this will apparently continue for several more weeks until the monsoon begins in July. This time of year is called the 'build-up' which is very descriptive of what actually happens. Each morning I wake up sweating, and as the day continues the humidity rises, encompassing Calcutta like a taut balloon, just waiting for the day when the balloon will finally burst and the rains begin. This never ending build-up is both physically and mentally draining. It makes life extremely difficult in the dispensary and I pour gallons of sweat all over the wounds I am treating. Fortunately it doesn't seem to do any harm.

Working here gives me a small feeling of achievement. The patient comes in, you diagnose and treat as best you can, and they leave a little better off. It's not life saving on the grand scale but it gives me the feeling of at least helping one person at a time.

Kalighat, on the other hand, often overwhelms me with the enormity of the problems facing Calcutta. Thirty per cent of patients admitted eventually die. The other seventy per cent are on the poverty treadmill. A cycle of acute illness and crisis following years of chronic disease and deprivation is played out every day at Kalighat. The beds are never empty and the new and more desperate arrivals claim priority over those fit enough for discharge back onto the streets. But with each afternoon I spend here, I become more at ease with the harsh reality of Indian life. Gone are my save-the-world fantasies; I now think it will be a miracle if I survive with my sanity intact.

The only thing missing in my life is some sort of social activity. I have always enjoyed the odd beer or dozen and am in my element at a wild and raucous party. The social agenda at the Y is centred around cups of coffee and deep, meaningful discussions about philosophy and religion. Fortunately for Weil and I, salvation comes in the form of an American girl named Maryanne. For some reason most Americans feel compelled to visit their embassy wherever they may be. She returns from her visit with the news that she has been invited to a party at the 'Marine House' on Friday night. Weil and I immediately volunteer to accompany her. Safety in numbers!

The next few days I spend daydreaming about my big night out. It feels like the first time I ever went to a party. The usual hassles of what to wear are restricted by the minute size of my wardrobe. Jeans, shirt and sandals will have to suffice.

Stepping from the taxi, we stare at the three-storeyed building before us. It just reeks of the West. The bricks and mortar somehow seem more secure. The grounds are well manicured and lush. The whole layout could have been transported here from the United States. Inside the door I first notice the air-conditioning, then the Western music, the smell of pizza and finally the bar. This is all my dreams come true. Of the fifty or so people present, eighty per cent are male. One of the marines claims Maryanne, so Weil and I swallow our nerves and head for the bar. Within minutes we each have a can of Heineken in one hand and a Benson and Hedges in the other. God is good.

The men Weil and I have fallen in with are mostly British. They are out here working for big steel companies or electricity stations. Their ages range from mid-thirties to sixties. Once we explain what we are doing in Calcutta and a little about the work, the guys take it upon themselves to be our guardian angels. They are just as lonely and frustrated in their work as we are and look forward to letting off a bit of steam at the weekends. We prove to be the novelty item of the night and, being in the minority, we are never short of a dance partner. There is nothing more ego-fulfilling than to be a woman surrounded by men. I meet marines, diplomats and businessmen and never once feel out of place. It is the first time in six weeks that I haven't felt like a foreigner.

After consuming several beers, my thoughts turn towards food. One of my guardian angels produces a menu and, with my mouth watering, I start with a BLT, several slices of pizza and French fries. The lads watch in consternation as I polish it all off and wash it down with yet another beer. I could die now and be in heaven! Weil is just as ravenous but being possessed of a little more maturity and experience she doesn't make a complete pig of herself. The night continues in grand style and the marines have offered an open invitation to return each Friday night. At midnight Norman and Alec drive us home to the Y, promising to pick us up on Sunday afternoon to go to the golf club. Norman and Alec are both English engineers and work for a large corporation called Davy Steel. Norman is based here for two years and Alec is out here for six weeks to check on progress at the plant. Norman is in his fifties. He has been here several months already and is a font of knowledge when it comes to the social activities available in Calcutta. We are extremely lucky that he has taken us under his wing and is prepared to introduce us to some of Calcutta's highlights. It seems amazing but I had completely forgotten about Calcutta while I was inside the marine compound.

*

Tollygunge Golf Club is on the outskirts of Calcutta. It has an eighteen-hole golf course, indoor and out-door swimming pools, squash and tennis courts, horse stables and horse racing. A large, white, sweeping building dominates the landscape as we come up the drive. Tables and chairs are placed under the bougainvillea and uniformed waiters maintain a hectic pace seeing to the needs of the members. Overseeing this whole enterprise is a British man by the name of Bob Wright. He is definitely a leftover from the Raj, his speech liberally sprinkled with 'well done' and 'super' along with many a 'jolly good show'. For once I am lost for words. The entire place evokes a feeling of stepping back in time. Crows calling in the trees are the only interruption to the tranquillity that encompasses the grounds. Chaos lives on the other side of the boundary wall and this is Paradise for as long as you stay.

I spend the afternoon swimming in the crystal-clear water of the pool. In the change rooms there are women employed to hand you towels and attend to your every need. I have no idea how to behave and feel guilty and self-conscious when they offer assistance.

This whole experience takes some sorting out. It is a fairytale existence and nothing in my middle-class background comes near to the extravagance and wealth on display here; my only entree into this society is my white skin. My socialist leanings are firmly shut away as I luxuriate in everything the club has to offer.

The boys take great delight in our obvious rapture and shock. Norman explains that this is one of many such clubs in Calcutta and that life for the well-off is one of servants and luxury. To think that this very morning I had been at Kalighat with the poorest of the poor and now I'm at the other end of the equation. Each end of the scale seems confident in its position. It's only we poor buggers in the middle that have trouble.

I shelve all deep and meaningful thoughts and give myself over to hedonistic pleasure. A wonderful item called steak toast is on the menu and I can't wait to try it. The plate before me looks like a steak sandwich, although Indian toast loses something in the translation and I have never seen this cut of meat before. I close my eyes and let my tastebuds enjoy themselves. A cold beer to wash this down and once again I'm lost in pleasure. The rest of the afternoon is spent around a table, drinking beer and telling tales in what is a time-honoured tradition, regardless of nationality.

 The monsoon is nearly upon us. I hope it provides some relief from this stifling humidity. Overhead fans make little impact and each morning I wake up covered in sweat. Volunteers are leaving in droves, heading out for the cooler climes. A handful remain, scattered around the various homes.

My unfortunate character flaw is to see any obstacle, either physical or mental, real or imagined, as a personal call to arms. This attitude has not proved very successful in the past, as any authority figure I have come into contact with will attest.

As luck will have it, though, it is a winner here. I have made it my mission in life to understand and conquer the transport and traffic systems of Calcutta. New horizons opened up when I discovered there was more than the No. 76 bus to Kalighat. I now have a choice between the 40a, 41b, 205, 13a and several mini-buses. Inside the bus I'm on the losing side at the moment, with my wallet having been stolen three times, but several painful blows for freedom from harassment have been struck along the way.

I prepare for the rain by making a mental note of where each and every manhole is located in my area.

According to the advice I've been given, the locals remove the covers in the belief that the water will run away faster. It is therefore imperative to know their locations. Dozens of people disappear down manholes each year. God, I love the challenge of living in this city!

I am spending most of my time at Kalighat these days and am even acknowledged by Sister Luke. Having passed her strict standards test, I have joined a very select group of her confidantes. She is from Singapore originally and is a trained nurse. Although her age is hard to judge, she would have to be somewhere in her early fifties. The more I work with her, the more the burdens and complexities of running this home become apparent. It is a constant juggling act between admissions and discharges.

Mind you, Sister Luke has a flair for drama. I have witnessed many Academy-Award-winning performances when she sets forth with the patients' records and attempts to cull the numbers. This always occurs in the mornings and most patients are alert to a sudden change in atmosphere. Men who were animated and chatty only minutes before are now moaning and groaning, shivering under their blankets in the mistaken belief that this will save them. No amount of pleading and wailing can reverse her decision, although it must be a heart-wrenching job to perform.

The women generally tend towards the invisible approach. They seem to shrink, becoming silent and unobtrusive, and thus can often escape detection. Each ejected person is given a new set of clothes, a blanket and 15 rupees as they leave. Medication is also provided to those with an ongoing need. Unfortunately the majority will be re-admitted at some stage in the future.

This morning Sister Luke is screaming her head off as I walk in the door. Apparently a patient is missing. What is even more disturbing is the possibility that this Muslim man has been inadvertently mistaken for a Hindu. Nobody seems sure about the status of the man; that is, whether he is dead or alive. As I try to pass by Sister Luke she grabs my arm and tells me to check the morgue.

'How am I supposed to find him? Ask him to stand up?' I ask.

'Don't be stupid,' she yells. 'Check the dead bodies and make sure that the Muslims and Hindus are not mixed up.'

'And how am I going to accomplish that?'

'Quite simple. Muslims are circumcised,' she informs me and then sweeps past.

I feel so much better now I have that sorted out. Approaching the doors of the morgue, I am unconvinced of my suitability for the job but have learnt never to argue with Sister Luke in one of these moods. The morgue is a basic cement and tile room about three metres square. The bodies are placed on two shelves on either side. The rule of thumb in here is 'Hindus on the left, Muslims on the right and Christians on top'. The only concession to refrigeration is an overhead fan which is rarely turned on. A small, framed quotation proclaiming, 'I'm on my way to heaven' adorns the far wall. Today there are several bodies in residence and each is wrapped in a thin white cotton sheet, tied at the head, middle and toes.

I have been in and out of this room on dozens of occasions and never greatly worried about it. Now I feel like some form of criminal, waiting for someone to tap me on the back and demand my reasons for being here. With trepidation and fingers shaking I part the sheet of the first person on the Hindu side and heave a sigh of relief on recognising one of the women. I'm starting with faces in the hope that recognition will make further investigation unnecessary. Unfortunately the next body is a man and he looks dreadfully similar to many that have passed before my eyes. Inhaling a deep breath, I inspect the poor man's genitals and justify his place on the left-hand benches. As quickly as possible I check the remaining six bodies and convince myself that everything is as it should be. There is one man I am not sure about, his genitals bearing the unmistakable marks of advanced syphilis, but the last thing I want to do is go out and ask for a second opinion. This has been too surreal already.

Escaping to the roof for a cigarette, I run into John, a Canadian volunteer. Dragging deeply on each calming breath of smoke, I tell him my problem. Inexplicably he collapses into fits of laughter. Several minutes later he informs me that Sister Luke found the missing Muslim ages ago. He was in the wrong bed, semi-conscious and covered with blankets. I storm down the stairs in search of the wretched woman, ready for blood. Sister Luke is crouched beside one of the beds. Standing up, she hands me a white sheet and says calmly, 'Here is our missing man.'

Once again I am back in the morgue. At least this time everyone is at rest.

The great panic over this man is all to do with burial practices; the Hindus are cremated, the Muslims buried and there is hell to pay if they are mixed up. Religion in India is a living organism, and trying to make sense of all the different customs, festivals, rituals and dietary habits of the various religions is a daily learning experience. Kalighat has its own little foibles and bizarre practices that can leave you wondering about which planet you have landed on. Living and working here in Calcutta is often like a 'Fawlty Towers' episode.

The morgue at Kalighat, where the line between the living and the dead was sometimes uncomfortably blurred

 Kalighat is once more in turmoil. Maria, the child of one of the workers, has a hole in the heart which requires corrective surgery. All the resources at our disposal are to be used to help Maria. By resources I don't mean money. I mean that a couple of volunteers will have to join the Indian hospital merry-go-round and find Maria a surgeon and a hospital bed. Nuns are the same the world over: they automatically believe that when they seriously want something, divine providence will deliver.

Two South African volunteers, Beverly and Shona, are the unlikely conscripts. The poor buggers have only been here a few weeks and their glowing idealism and zeal is about to be sorely tested. Fortunately for me, I am to remain here at Kalighat and assist the girls with my knowledge of the system, and help in my free time. Don't you just love nuns?

Hospitals in Calcutta are large, overcrowded, filthy and crumbling places. As luck will have it, our local hospital has a cardiac unit, although I've been to the P.G. Hospital on several occasions and have never felt safe leaving a patient there. Most of my trips have been to the out-patients department, where I have unashamedly used every trick at my disposal for the betterment of my charge. White skin can move mountains and is certainly an asset in circumventing a mile-long queue. I have also discovered that female volunteers have better results at the hospital than their male counterparts. A friendly chat over a cup of tea can induce some young doctors to perform wonders of modern medicine for your patient. Beverly and Shona are very sceptical of this approach and their limited racial interactions don't promise much. I know that I have been around Sister Luke too long when I hear myself say, 'Don't worry about yourselves, just do your best for Maria.'

Another useful tool is the art of barter. Enormous quantities of medicines and supplies are donated to Mother Teresa. Hundreds of boxes arrive from England, France, Germany, Sweden, Belgium, Ireland, Japan, Canada, the US, and even Russia, and the volunteers are always used to interpret and categorise these treasured gifts. Any medication or equipment that comes from the West is automatically given superior status to the Indian equivalent. This practice is even more pronounced among the Indians themselves.

The boxes are something of a lucky dip. While looking for the essentials, such as antibiotics, anti-malarials, paracetamol, anti-parasitics etc., a whole box of anti-depressants or tranquillisers might be found—more use to the staff than to the patients. The equipment supplied is usually IV sets, syringes and needles, catheters, scalpels, and boxes and boxes of gloves (none of which we ever seem to use). Surprises in the equipment line can be some of the more complicated and exotic appliances used in most intensive care wards of the Western world. Shona and Beverly should be able to find plenty of the medication and equipment needed for the treatment of Maria and offer some other goodies in exchange for the bits they can't find. They are horrified by the whole process but are learning fast.

*

The girls are working wonders. In just a couple of weeks they have found a surgeon, Professor Sen Gupta. Upon hearing the name 'Mother Teresa' he gave a resigned smile and offered his services free of charge. The poor man has undoubtedly come in contact with the irresistible force before. Most medical and governmental establishments have had dealings with Mother in the past and her reputation for dogged persistence and a take-no-prisoners attitude reduces even the most feared bureaucratic despot to a quivering mess. It's great to be able to call upon this power—almost like being part of the Mafia. The funny part is that Mother Teresa is not even in the country and knows nothing of the operation anyway. Sister Luke is hopeless at intimidation outside Kalighat, which is why she sends volunteers on most hospital trips. My philosophy is to use all weapons at our disposal.

P.G. Hospital will provide free theatre services and a ward bed. Beverly has developed a friendship with the cardiac registrar, much to her surprise. He is a lovely guy and more than willing to assist in this venture. He has even discovered some excellent heart medicines in the donation boxes.

A sterile piece of tubing for the bypass machine is the only thing still needed for the operation, so Sister Berchmans and I are instructed to go and purchase this item. She sits comfortably in the front of the ambulance with the driver, while I am relegated to the back. This ambulance looks like something used by the Germans during the Second World War. It is all sharp corners and chunky. Painted in the traditional blue and white colours of the Missionaries of Charity, it cuts quite a swathe through the Calcutta traffic. The cavernous interior is furnished with two long and narrow wooden bench seats. Sister Berchmans dispenses with the usual recitation of the rosary and instead keeps up a steady litany on the shortcomings of Calcutta's traffic and its many drivers. She also shares her views freely with several other road users, much to their amusement. None of this seems to hasten our progress but it keeps her happy.

Two hours later we stop in front of a small, ramshackle building with a faded sign advertising medical supplies. To the uninitiated, Calcutta may appear a completely disorganised city, but each industry or specialty is located in a specific area and medical supplies just happen to be on the other side of the city from Kalighat. Sister Berchmans marches in with me trailing in her wake. She hands the man a slip of paper and he disappears through a curtain. We wait. Thirty minutes later he reappears clasping a small plastic packet. I can't believe that anything sterile could be housed in such a filthy little shop. As I inspect it and verify that it is indeed the tubing we need, I also closely examine it to reassure myself that it is still sealed inside its dusty outer covering. With my nod of approval Sister Berchmans reluctantly opens her bag and counts out 2300 rupees. This is about A\$230. The poor woman nearly faints as she passes the money over, but manages several words in Bengali that I am certain are not taught in any good Catholic school. Mission successful, we return to Kalighat triumphant.

The operation is only one day away now. Beverly and Shona have accomplished a mammoth feat. The only thing missing is four bags of blood. It is over breakfast at the Y that Beverly drops this piece of information. She is quick to inform me that this will not be a problem as *we* can exchange our own blood for the type we need. As Shona has drawn the line at this idea, I am the only sucker left. Beverly's idealism is also wearing very thin and she tends to see me as the devil incarnate for getting her involved in the first place. With a guilty conscience I agree to accompany Beverly to the Assembly of God Hospital and donate my blood. As Indian hospitals go, the A.G. is among the best of them. It is reasonably clean and well run. Unfortunately for Maria it is not a public hospital and only accepts a few charity cases.

We enter the blood bank area and are greeted warmly by the doctor in charge. He gives us a guided tour of his primitive but clean domain. A technician escorts Beverly and I into a room with two beds and asks us to lie down. As I recline, I offer a short but fervent prayer to God and all his offsiders that this will not prove to be one of the more stupid things I have done. With anxious eyes, I inspect all the equipment around me and am reassured that sterility is to be maintained and the needle to be used is new. The technician tightens the tourniquet. His technique is individual, to say the least. Having secured the tourniquet he starts patting around for a vein. After one pat on the breast I give him the benefit of the doubt but on the fourth occasion I redirect his attention (none too politely) to the bulging veins in my arm.

Fifteen minutes later my contribution is completed and we are treated to a feast of coffee, biscuits and bananas. The doctor then presents us with cards detailing our blood group and carrying the message 'You have just saved a precious human life' printed in large block letters. He then asks if we would like to meet the patients that are to receive our blood and Beverly and I are swept along on this amazingly absurd blood-swap experience. God, this place is unreal.

My young man is delighted to be receiving strong, healthy Western blood. The psychological effect alone seems to revitalise him. I'm beside myself with delusions of heroism until I reach Kalighat, where Sister Luke delivers multiple blows to my head as she calls me every name in the book, convincing me that I now harbour every blood-borne disease known to man. Nuns can be so deflating.

The morning sees Beverly, Shona and I bright and early outside the P.G. Hospital. With trepidation we mount the stairs to the operating theatre. I close my mind to the dirt and decay in the stairwell and try to maintain positive thoughts. Entering the theatre area a staff nurse approaches and hands us clean theatre gowns. When I start to remove my street clothes she nearly has a nervous breakdown. With much gesturing and loud protestation, she indicates she wants us to use the gowns over our street clothes. My hopes of a successful outcome for Maria plunge even further as I realise that our filthy thongs and sandals are deemed suitable to wear into the theatre. God only knows how many germs we are carrying in there. Thankfully most Indians are bred tough and have robust immune systems; anyway we've got all those lovely Western antibiotics if all else fails.

The theatre itself is a large room of the standard green-tiled variety. There are many chipped and missing tiles along with a stained ceiling. On the whole, though, it possesses the useful bits of machinery common to operating theatres. All the players are here and while Maria is prepared for surgery we adjourn next-door for a cup of tea. Professor Sen Gupta is in fine form and doesn't anticipate any problems. As we wander back into the theatre it strikes me as quite bizarre that Beverly, Shona and I will be witnessing our first ever open-heart surgery in these basic surroundings so far from home. They also trained in a small regional hospital and cases such as this were always sent to the big cities. Fortunately for Maria, the other people in the theatre have performed this operation numerous times before. Within a short space of time Professor Sen Gupta has located and closed the hole which was causing all the trouble. Once Maria is off bypass and her heart is beating soundly, the professor hands over to his registrar and bids us all goodbye.

When the operation is finally completed and Maria is in recovery, I experience a sort of emotional let-down. The excitement and intrigue of the past week is at an end. I return to Kalighat and relay the news of a successful operation to the family and sisters. It makes a change to be part of a group that actually accomplishes something in the medical jungle of Calcutta.

 During the last few months I have had the most wonderful, if at times exhausting, social life. Every Friday night has seen me in full flight at the Marine House. Thursdays are also significant for the fact that it is a dry day, when no alcohol is to be served in Calcutta. It is also a meatless day, although chicken somehow makes it onto the menu.

Whenever human beings are told not to do something it only seems to inflame the desire. As a result, Thursdays find me alighting from the bus two stops earlier on my return from Kalighat and making my way to Ho Chi Minh Sarani and the British High Commission bar. All the lads are gathered here and from 6.30 p.m. till 9.00 p.m. we have a few beers and play darts. The bar is open every night of the week but most of us only attend on a Thursday. After closing, the boys draw straws to see who will take me out to dinner. My voracious appetite is now legendary and whoever gets the short straw wins the pleasure of my company. I keep reminding them that keeping me fed and watered is their contribution to the humanitarian work of Mother Teresa. Like most Poms they love nothing more than teasing an Australian, but I thank my lucky stars for the sanity and normality they have brought to my life here. I don't think I could hack it on my own. Many volunteers come with high hopes and aspirations only to be defeated by Calcutta and their unreal expectations of themselves. My men help me lead a wonderful double life, working with the poor during the day and partying with the rich at night. This type of logic fits very easily in Calcutta.

The majority of these men are on short-term assignments and as they pass the reins to the next man they also pass on my name and room number with instructions to make sure that I am taken out to dinner regularly.

It is mixing with the Thursday crowd that sees me invited to the screening of the royal wedding. I had no intention of going until an English girl, Catherine, implored me to take her. We fronted up at the British Embassy on the day to have pre-wedding drinks and appetisers in the garden. This time I really did feel out of place but Catherine was in her element and patriotically looking forward to the wedding. The royal family has never played a large part in my life. The film rolled through, with all due ceremony maintained until the end, and then we pretended that we were all at the reception and drank endless toasts to Charles and Di and every other member of the family. Awaking with yet another hangover the next day, I smiled and thought that only in Calcutta could I be invited to the royal wedding and reception. God, I love this place.

The sisters have taken a motherly interest in my nocturnal pursuits and wait with bated breath for my reports of the previous night's activities. Most of them have never experienced the sort of freedom and abandonment that I describe and they always wait until the end of my tale before starting the standard lectures on the evils of men and alcohol. They get much enjoyment out of trying to save me.

I have been invited to the annual Marines' Ball. This is the absolute pinnacle of the social calendar. It is to be held in the grand ballroom of the Oberoi Grand Hotel. The dress code is black tie and ball gowns. Herein lies my problem—the age-old cry of 'I have nothing to wear'. Sister Luke and Sister Berchmans take this catastrophic situation to heart and start describing all manner of wild and wonderful creations. An American girl, Patty, is with me and she is also in need of a dress, but as we listen to the nuns talk of sequins and lace, visions of garishness float before us. Unfortunately the Kalighat genie is already out of the bottle. Within minutes, Patty and I are in the back of the ambulance, with Sister Berchmans directing our progress towards the New Market.

Sister Berchmans is a native of Calcutta and has refined the process of bargaining down to an art form. We follow her meekly through the maze that is the market area. To the uninitiated, the markets are an incomprehensible mixture of every known animate and inanimate object on the face of the planet. Covering an entire city block, the narrow passageways and tiny nooks and crannies compound to confuse and disorient the unwary. Sister Berchman's march towards the fabric section is unwavering. Patty and

I are overcome with the seemingly limitless choice available.

Sister Berchmans makes her way into a small store and deposits herself in the only chair available. She issues several instructions to the shopkeeper and dozens of bolts of material are removed from shelves and laid out for our inspection. All these materials are silk and of gorgeous quality. Patty and I have decided to have Punjabi dresses made and we will require two colours for each outfit. Needless to say, our choice of design does not meet with the good sister's approval. Fortunately for us she is on her own and for once we have the upper hand. Patty chooses a cream silk for the overdress and brown for the pants. I really splash out and choose a shiny, silver-patterned silk for the dress and a light, black silk for my pants. Despite Sister Berchmans' disappointment at our lack of colour sense and style, she devotes herself whole-heartedly to the task of settling the price. Within ten minutes the poor cloth merchant is in tears, pleading poverty and starvation for his family. The final act is played out with her threatening hellfire and damnation unless the wreck of a man agrees to 30 rupees a metre for the tops and 15 rupees a metre for the bottoms. Patty and I have shamefully hidden ourselves during this exchange, cringing with every blow delivered on our behalf. At $3 and $1.50 a metre we realise we have a terrific bargain so we quickly pay up and make a hasty exit from the markets.

Back at Kalighat our purchases are roundly condemned for their lack of imagination and within minutes alternative designs and ideas are discussed.

The sequins and lace are once again mentioned. Patty and I follow the progress of our material along the female aisle; all interest is now centred around the sewing lady. This is one of the Indian workers who daily pedals her machine while repairing sheets and making pyjamas and other garments. I am really starting to worry now. Imagine turning up at the ball, having someone ask you where you had your dress made and replying, 'Oh! The home for the dying and destitute.' Patty and I rescue our material as diplomatically as possible and, professing our thanks and blessings to the sisters, make our way hastily back to the Y. We find a street full of dressmakers and, after much deliberation, we leave our material with a man sitting on the floor of his tiny shop next to his sewing machine. He seems to understand what we want but in this very confusing city that could mean anything. Time for a little faith again.

A week later the dresses have been made and Patty and I are to show them off at Kalighat. Once there, we decide to model them ourselves. My outfit has loose black pyjama pants gathered at the ankles, and a three-quarter length overdress. This is of the silver-patterned material; it has a Chinese-type collar and three-quarter length sleeves. The dress itself is quite a snug fit and has slits up either side for ease of movement. I am delighted with it as I think it looks quite glamorous while still feeling comfortable. Sister Luke still thinks it lacks a certain sparkle, but fortunately she is too late to do any great harm. Patty's dress is a similar style in brown and cream. The patients of Kalighat are just as anxious as the sisters and workers to participate in our adventures, so Patty and I stage our very own fashion show. As we parade up and down the aisle on the male ward, the men offer all manner of advice and suggestions along with the standard whistles. I only hope that no tourists walk in at this moment expecting to see the angels of God tending the poorest of the poor. As we move on to the female ward the women offer sighs of appreciation; many want to feel the material and offer their own fashion advice. It is like belonging to one big family, with Sister Luke and Sister Berchmans as the parents and the other sisters, workers and patients as the siblings. The only thing lacking is the lecture, and this Sister Luke delivers as we prepare to leave. Don't drink too much and watch out for the men: I have heard different versions of the same theme from my mother for many years.

Arriving at the Grand Hotel and entering the ballroom through the marine guard of honour is like something out of Cinderella. The room is a vision of marble floors and chandeliers with hundreds of exotic flowers in every corner. Of course my eye is immediately taken by the buffet table and the delights that await me there. My obsession with food shows no sign of diminishing. All the marines are in their dress blue uniforms, complete with swords which add even more drama to the occasion. My date for the evening is Colin, a Scottish engineer. He is here on a short contract and lives in fear of the teeming millions and the threat of disease. He considers me completely mad to voluntarily come to this place. Several other volunteers are also here and my friend Norman informs me that it is very simple to pick us out. How? I ask him. He tells an enthralled audience that we all scratch. As I watch the other girls, I realise that we have indeed become so accustomed to the itch of scabies that we all unconsciously scratch with great regularity. Obviously it is nothing that a few drinks won't fix.

The entire night lives up to my expectations of food, drinks, dancing and great fun. I'm still going strong at 5.00 a.m. and join a few other diehards for a breakfast of bacon and eggs at the Marine House. I eventually reach my bed at No. 18 around 7.00 a.m. and collapse for the rest of the day.

The next day at Kalighat sees me giving a detailed, if somewhat censored, account of the night to all interested parties. The sisters love the whole fairytale story, while the men like to focus more on the alcohol and general debauchery. Only in Kalighat can so many people enjoy one person's night out!

 Many books have been written about Mother Teresa and her work and they all seem to describe Kalighat in some ethereal fashion. In *Something Beautiful for God,* Malcolm Muggeridge portrays it in quite mystical terms; for instance, he describes a divine light streaming through the windows. I can only believe that he must have been there on one of the many days when the stove has blown up and the entire place has been shrouded in smoke.

To me, Kalighat often resembles photos I have seen of World War I field hospitals. It is a brutal and demanding place where the results of man's inhumanity to man eventually end up. Not only are patients admitted with disease-related problems, many find their way here after acts of violence have been committed against them. Some of the saddest cases are those of young beggars, usually intellectually disabled, who have had hot oil thrown in their faces by shopkeepers anxious to move them on. It is the callous treatment of these and many others in Calcutta which often leads you to despair of anything ever changing here. To see a human being brought in with barely a centimetre of skin left intact on his back and legs, maggots infesting his flesh, and to know that only hours previously other people walked over him and around him without a second glance is enough to make you wonder if this society deserves to survive. But the philosophy of the Missionaries of Charity centres on the man, not the cause, and his care and comfort are the reasons for their existence. Working at Kalighat leaves little time for reflection and it is only late in the evenings that I ever find the time to ponder the eternal questions of life. Then all I want to do is go out and hit someone! Fortunately the four bus trips a day to and from work provide ample opportunity to relieve my pent-up aggression.

Since my foray into the morgue some time ago, I have often been deputised to inspect the inhabitants and make sure that all are present and correct. Today as I check the bodies, a movement on the second shelf on the left-hand side almost has me joining the residents of the right-hand side. With my heart pounding in my ears and the ever-present sweat turned to ice, I tentatively reach for the offending sheet. My fingers are shaking so badly I can barely untie the knot.

I recognise the man and immediately realise he is still alive, if only just. Storming from the morgue I feel nothing but rage. The brothers are my targets and the first poor bugger that I see cops the full brunt of my attack. I use every foul and demeaning word I have ever heard and only fall short of physical abuse because Sister Luke drags me off him. Needless to say, she also starts yelling once I have calmed down enough to inform her of my discovery. We rescue the poor man from the morgue and remove his shroud only to discover that there is no bed for him. Sister Luke then performs the Kalighat shuffle and the person deemed least sick is ejected to make way for this man. His condition is critical and it will only be a matter of hours before he makes a return journey, but for now he is safe under the statue of Our Lady.

I need several cigarettes on the roof before I am calm enough to face the brothers again. It has been part of my work here to instruct and educate the brothers in basic nursing care. They have no academic or practical training before they are let loose on the patients, either here or at the other homes. While this place is far from being described as an acute care medical facility, I have tried to stress to the brothers and sisters that our goal should at least be to cause no harm.

Gathering the brothers around me an hour later I ask the all-important question: 'How do you tell if somebody is dead?' The general consensus among them seems to be that the person has to be cold and not moving. My hands bury themselves in my hair in an effort to prevent them from strangling one of the brothers. With more patience than I ever knew I possessed, I carefully explain the rudimentary function of the heart and the lungs. They find this highly amusing and inform me that of course they know all that. At this stage I explode and yell, 'Well then, why didn't you bloody well check them on this patient?' I take them all back down to the man in question and with the aid of a stethoscope ask them to check his heartbeat. As fate would have it, one look at the man tells me that we are already too late; however, the first brother happily reports a heartbeat. I nearly rip his head off as I grab the stethoscope. There is no heartbeat except in the brother's imagination. He is just being typically Indian and supplying the answer he thinks I want. Once again I give a detailed list of the signs of death and demonstrate each one, all the while thinking: I will only find out how successful this lecture has been when next I am on morgue patrol.

The only person remotely pleased with this final turn of events is the man selected for discharge. His eyes are glowing with the prospect of regaining his bed.

The sisters are in the same situation as the brothers. They are all young girls, mainly from the south of India, and consequently speak no Bengali and only a little English. They come to Kalighat on a rotation basis in three-month blocks. Just when I feel I have made headway with one group, their time is finished and the next incompetent lot arrive. The innocence and naivety of the sisters is compounded by their religious induction into a 'Leave it to Jesus' philosophy. Unfortunately, Jesus is not the one giving out the medications or administering injections to the patients. He, I would trust to get it right, but his helpers here have a lackadaisical approach to matters medical. I have seen them give the steroid Prednisone instead of paracetamol in the mistaken belief that they must be similar if they both start with the letter 'p'. Whenever I yell at them and accuse them of murdering the patients they simply smile and tell me that it is all in God's hands. I now understand the reason for Sister Luke's frequent verbal eruptions.

The young sisters' paramount interest is my personal life. It is quite amusing to be lectured on the evils of alcohol and men by seventeen-year-old girls fresh from the village. They see me as a lost soul in need of saving. They all hang on every word of my somewhat embellished stories—these young novices learn more from me than just medicine!—before delivering a sermon on evil. Of prime concern to them is my seeming lack of religion. Volunteers are judged on their piety by the frequency of their attendance at the Mother House for mass in the morning and adoration at night. Aside from my visits when I first arrived, the Mother House hasn't featured in my social calendar.

The only mass I attend is the one held every Sunday at Kalighat. The treatment table is transformed into

Tracey with some of Kalighat's young graduate sisters

an altar and mats are placed on the floor for the congregation. The hustle and bustle of everyday life continues around this celebration. It is the most meaningful ceremony I have ever attended. To be perched on the side of a patient's bed while he dies during mass is a moving experience. The madness of Kalighat also enters the picture, with patients yelling out and the usual mayhem of lunch being served at the same time, but this only adds to the reality of the situation. You can be drifting in thought when the person in the bed on which you sit decides to haemorrhage violently from his TB-infested lungs and shower you with blood. It all leads to a deeper celebration of life for me.

The sisters' adherence to dogma and rules makes it hard for them to understand my more relaxed approach to religion, but my being here gives them a chance to practise the art of salvation and redemption. Every three months I have to face a fresh onslaught and I get wicked enjoyment out of shocking the new recruits.

ELEVEN

 I have been here for four months now and the stresses of living in Calcutta and working at Kalighat are starting to take their toll. I have survived the monsoon season and rarely missed a day at work. Wading through the knee-deep water while trying to hold my breath for fear of inhaling the noxious fumes rising from the stagnant pools of refuse almost convinced me to give up smoking so as to increase my lung capacity. Within days of the rains beginning I adapted to the new wet conditions and barely registered the bloated, furry objects floating past. Rats are such a common part of the landscape that, alive or dead, their presence is taken for granted. As the senses go, it is the poor old nose that cops the unending assaults. I blindly walk through all manner of filth and don't even look for the source of particularly offensive objects until my nose starts running and my lungs constrict. It is only when something out of the ordinary happens that I even stop and realise that I am becoming desensitised to the hell in which I live.

This whole environment is having a detrimental effect on my psyche. To begin with, the humidity is so energy sapping that just getting to and from work each day is a monumental effort. Then there is the work itself. Every person needs to feel appreciated and to have their efforts acknowledged. Working at Kalighat is the ultimate in ego abuse. You begin with the idealism and inner glow of helping your fellow man, only to discover that the internal fire needs to be stoked every so often or it burns out. My resources are at an all-time low, with both physical and mental exhaustion ready to knock me out.

I have suffered numerous bouts of diarrhoea since being here; in fact I have come to the conclusion that I will never see a formed stool again! Constipation and laxatives are a peculiarly Western affliction. My diet now includes an omelette each morning and an odd mixture of fruit, bread and biscuits along with my saviour, Vegemite. I always make up for lost calories whenever one of the boys takes me out. Calcutta is teaching me many things, paramount among them is learning to eat most dishes put in front of me. My mother will be amazed when I return and she sees me eating vegetables and eggs.

Depression is a very easy trap to fall into here. The futility of working in a place like Kalighat becomes clearer the longer you stay. It is only over several months that you can recognise the same faces returning, one step closer to joining the 30 per cent. A burning desire to save these regulars can be soul-destroying. They belong to the Kalighat family as much as do the workers, sisters and volunteers, and are part of the fabric of the home. I occasionally run into one of the ex-Kalighat crowd on the streets and try to supply food and medicine where needed. It is like old home week when one of my ex-patients recognises me and we stop and natter away like old friends, much to the disgust of the surrounding crowd. Middle- and lower-class Indians frown on fraternisation with the untouchables. Eventually, though, everyone returns to Kalighat in one form or another. Life is just too hard for those with chronic illness to fight against it.

The brutality of life and the realities of existence for the poor do not, as many writers would have you believe, create a class of people more willing to share and band together. There is nothing noble or uplifting about being poor. Survival of the fittest and smartest is the governing rule at the bottom of the heap as well as at the top. Most patients admitted here are street smart and, depending on their degree of illness, will always be on the lookout for the main chance. Food is the most common item for hoarding and bartering. Well-to-do Indians often come to Kalighat and distribute sweets and pastries. This is part of the Hindu tradition of giving alms to the poor. Some patients trade these with the workers for cigarettes and other favours. The occasional volunteer will also fall prey to one of the more polished con-men and end up parting with hundreds of rupees. This is not very common but sometimes the pure gullibility of the volunteer is too much of a temptation for the patient. I must admit to also preying on the naivety of volunteers to satisfy my own twisted sense of humour. There are ex-volunteers wandering the globe convinced that their contribution of American cigarettes really did make it to Mother Teresa's own lips.

I am seriously considering going home to Australia. It is all becoming too much to cope with. I haven't really been homesick since I've been here, and on the whole it has been a great adventure. The cause of my depression is general physical exhaustion, feeling unappreciated, and the really big one—my twenty-first birthday next week. There is nothing like self-pity to make you long for safety and normality; Kalighat is not an ideal place in which to be depressed. This last week has seen me arriving at work lethargic and just going through the motions once there.

This afternoon I am alone on the male ward as all the sisters are on retreat. In robot fashion and without my usual good humour I dispense the food and medications, trying to keep my temper in check while everyone seems to cry out for attention at the same time. In my present frame of mind, murder is not a remote possibility. The patients sense my mood and try as much as possible to assist me in the work. Among the many prostrate bodies lying under their blankets I discover a new admission who has somehow managed to find a bed but has had no treatment at all. Once again it is my nose that leads the way in detecting this man's problems. The pungent, sickly sweet smell of gangrenous flesh is something I have learnt to identify over the months.

The patient, an old, grey-haired man, is far from happy when I try to remove his blanket to check him out. His only concern at the moment is to wrap himself in the blanket and sleep. After a cautious search, I discover a filthy, rotting bandage on his leg. The sight of maggots and the overpowering smell of decaying flesh are something that I will never get used to. Every time I'm confronted with them I want to throw up.

I prepare a dressing tray and return to treat his wound. As I lean over and remove the putrid bandage, the old guy lets fly with his other leg and connects with my chest, sending me flying through the air and landing two beds away. Fortunately the man on whom I land doesn't seem to mind and just smiles at me sweetly. In the hushed surroundings a lone patient arises, walks over to the man, delivers a blow to his head, sits on his chest and then says, 'Carry on, mem-sahib.' I nearly break down and cry. My saviour is Budhamin Rai and he is afflicted with a cancerous growth covering most of his head. Movement of any kind is extremely painful for him and the effort involved for him to walk, let alone punch, is monumental. All of my real and imagined problems and worries are blown away by his selfless act of kindness. His beaming smile grows even brighter as the other patients applaud his show of force. I quickly attend to the wound and return the old man to his blanket cocoon. My main concern is to help Budhamin back to his bed. His heroic acts have taken their toll and he is very pale and sweaty.

Having settled Budhamin in his bed, I search the medicine cupboard for the strongest painkillers I can find. Miraculously I find a bottle of pethidine tablets and remove several of these. Strong narcotics are seldom dispensed at Kalighat, not because the patients don't suffer great pain but because they rarely complain. My discovery of the pethidine tablets will at least help ease the excruciating pain Budhamin now suffers. Sitting beside his bed, I give him two tablets and leave four under his pillow for the night. We then share a cigarette and I thank him once again for all his help. Budhamin Rai is Nepalese and has the most beautiful smile; it seems to light his whole face. He knows that he is going to die and that his journey will be extremely painful, but with an acceptance and lightness of spirit he is eager for his next life. Maybe the belief in reincarnation helps him face death with some measure of serenity. All I know is that his actions have brought new life and meaning to me. One heroic gesture has turned my muddled mind around and shown me what is really important in life. I still have a lot to learn from the people here, it is just a matter of recognising the teachers.

TWELVE

 I have decided to give myself a weekend off work and to celebrate my birthday in style. Leaving Kalighat this evening I received many birthday wishes and a pointed talk from Sister Luke on the practice of moderation and restraint. As I shower and change, ready for a night at the Marine House, the only thoughts in my head are of party and fun. This weekend is all mine and I intend to live every moment of it to the fullest.

Together with several other girls from the Y, I descend on the marines and get down to some serious partying. Within minutes we have shed our Indian personae and are once again normal Westerners attending an ordinary party. This chameleon-like existence is the same for everybody here. It makes no difference whether we are European, American or Australian as we all share a reasonably common cultural background. We also share the white skin phenomenon so, while we are just part of the norm in our own societies, we are markedly foreign in Calcutta. It is a remarkable learning experience to be singled out and judged by your pigmentation alone. Fortunately the discrimination is positive and the only real drawbacks are loss of anonymity and privacy. It is a real luxury to be in a group of people without feeling self-conscious.

The night is spent dancing, drinking, eating and talking. We are groups of individuals who would normally never mix socially and yet the common thread of Calcutta binds us together. We can give each other hope and support, even though we don't necessarily understand each other's field of work. The sole aim of these 'Thank God it's Friday' parties is to let your hair down and forget all about the outside world.

I finally make it back to the Y about 2.00 a.m., having consumed more bottles of beer than I care to remember, eaten enough food to last a poor family a month and smoked at least a packet of cigarettes. As I weave my way to good old No. 18 I judge the evening to have been an outstanding success. Amazingly I even remember not to set the alarm for the morning.

*

God, I hate the morning after. I am definitely going to reform one day. Waking at 10.00 a.m., I almost have a heart attack thinking I'm late for work. Sinking my pounding head back onto the pillow, my brain finally reminds the rest of me that today is all mine, to do with it what I will. This in itself is one of the greatest gifts I can receive. I realise I have painted myself into a corner at Kalighat. My habit of going to work every day at the same time has built up Sister Luke's expectations, so that if I miss a day she sarcastically asks if I have had a good holiday! It is, after all, only a voluntary job, but nuns and guilt go hand in hand.

Freshly showered and clothed, I can now face the day. There are no other volunteers wandering around the Y this morning, and over a refreshing cup of coffee I decide to head to the one place in Calcutta that I know will offer both sanctuary and sustenance. Packing swimming trunks and a book I stride purposefully up Park Street and onto a bus. The omens for the day are wonderful if this half-empty bus is any indication. Thirty minutes later I am enveloped in the serenity of the Tollygunge Golf Club. During the next two hours I swim, sunbathe, read and drowse by the pool. My mind is clear and my body feels positively sparkling. It is always a bit embarrassing to look at my dirt encrusted feet which no amount of scrubbing seems to improve. A good soaking in the pool has done the trick and they are now fit for polite society. With batteries recharged, I wander over to the 18th shamiana in the hope that Norman or another of the boys will be there. As I am not a member here, I can't sign for any drinks or food and without a member to sign me in I can't buy any chits, even if I had the money. I vaguely remember that last night Norman told me he would be here playing golf today. Since meeting Norman at the Marine House all those weeks ago, I've decided he is the nicest, most generous man I have ever met. He has about eighteen months of his two-year contract still to run, and is well established in an apartment in Calcutta. He has a daughter a few years older than me, and his wife lives at home in England. It is great to sit around listening to his stories and to watch him proudly showing around photographs of his grandchildren. He is like an older brother to me and can be just as over-protective.

The good omens are holding as I reach the 18th shamiana and spot Norman and his group holing out on the green. Once they have showered and changed, we sit around the table and begin again on the food and beer cycle. My actual birthdate is tomorrow and when the others realise that it is my twenty-first, they respond in the appropriate manner. The world is my oyster and my every wish is their command. During the next three or four hours, each and every one of my champions regales me with stories of his twenty-first party, complete with subsequent hangover and any other items of interest he can remember. With the mosquitoes attacking our legs, it suddenly dawns on us that the night has crept up on us. Unable to decide on a place to go, we do the next best thing and move inside to the airconditioned bar. We spend several more hours discussing the relative merits of every bar, restaurant, nightclub and other private club in Calcutta. It is only when the bar shuts down at 10.00 p.m. that further movement is forced upon us. Six people fit quite comfortably into Norman's Indian-made Ambassador car and, as we careen around the streets, the profound thought strikes me that Calcutta's traffic should always be faced in a completely intoxicated condition. I am feeling absolutely no pain and no fear, even in the face of the mayhem rushing around and past us. Norman obviously has the same confidence and within minutes he has us parked in the garage at his apartment. We fall out of the car and make our way upstairs.

Norman's apartment is a fairly modern one with a lovely balcony area off the living room, two bedrooms, bathroom, kitchen and dining area. It has a nice homely feel to it and could be an apartment anywhere in the world. Relaxing in the comfortable chairs, our riotous assembly soon seems to be running out of steam. Within a couple of hours the pace and length of our celebrations start to take their toll. After one last round of 'Happy Birthday', Norman offers me the use of his spare room and bundles the others off into a taxi. This is the first time I have ever stayed here and it is with selfish delight that I savour the clean sheets and peace and quiet. The prospect of a hot bath in the morning leaves a smile of anticipation on my face as my head hits the pillow.

I wake bright and refreshed around 8.00 a.m. and after a luxurious soak in the bath emerge to discover a culinary miracle occurring in the kitchen. Norman has a cook/housekeeper and this marvellous young man can perform wonders with food. This morning he has wished me a happy birthday, ushered me to a seat, and then placed in front of me a plate of bacon, scrambled eggs, grilled tomato and toast. I feel like I have died and gone to heaven. No wonder Norman has trouble with his girth, living in this paradise. I even read the Sunday paper with a cup of coffee after demolishing the delicious breakfast. Norman drives me back to the Y—and reality—as he heads back to Tollygunge for yet more golf.

Outside the door of No. 18 is a plastic bucket with flowers in it. The card informs me that they are from Naveen. He and Eskay are men that I met in the corner coffee shop. I have been out with both of them several times, and since I explained that sex was not on the agenda they have been just as happy to have me accompany them to dinner and nightclubs and let all their friends assume they are raging studs. They are both married and are relatively well off. The nightlife in Calcutta is nearly exclusively male, as most decent Indian girls would not be allowed out without the family. Naveen and Eskay have taken me to dozens of restaurants and clubs all over the city. It has certainly been an education and we have developed quite a friendship.

I deposit all my things in the room and wander downstairs to the dining room for another cup of coffee. As I issue a hale and hearty good morning to all present I detect a decidedly frosty response. What have I done wrong now? They demand to know where I have been all night. It transpires that they had planned a surprise birthday party for me last night, but as I didn't turn up, they sat around worrying about me instead. To say the least, I am not on the top of anyone's hit parade this morning, particularly in my annoyingly chipper state. Thankfully the animosity is short-lived; we are soon back upstairs where I open several presents. It is especially wonderful for me to be celebrating my birthday amongst friends from all over the world. Friendships made here seem to be forged with a strength that can only occur in the stressful and difficult place in which we live. Shared experience unites, as does the feeling that only other volunteers can really appreciate the kind of life we lead. I wouldn't want to be anywhere else in the world right now.

I nearly keel over when Catherine tells me that she has arranged to take me to lunch at the Tollygunge Club. It is starting to feel like my second home. An Indian friend of hers has volunteered to drive us out there. Refinement is the order of the day for this particular visit to Tollygunge. We move straight into the dining room where I try to keep my head lowered and away from the many waiters who witnessed yesterday's marathon session. My new lady-like pretensions are almost undone when the drinks waiter enquires after my health. He walks away, quietly laughing to himself and shaking his head. His intimate knowledge of my birthday was another bit of a slip. Most Indians tend to ignore the staff, but during my time here I've exchanged personal information with half the waiters and even conducted a semi-clinic in the bathroom for the women working at the club. I've heard about every disease and illness visited upon these people and their families and supplied diagnosis and treatment wherever I can. God only knows what they make of me.

Lunch is going along fairly well until I try to eat a piece of steak while talking, and it lodges in my throat. As the lack of oxygen turns my face an ever-deepening shade of red, I notice my luncheon companions staring at me with increasing horror and panic. I quickly realise that no useful assistance will be gained from that quarter so, as demurely as possible, I place my fingers down my throat and let nature expel the offending article into my napkin. If only my companions had behaved in a less hysterical manner no-one would have noticed anything amiss. The incident did, however, cause me to remember the numerous prophecies of my school teachers that I would either be dead or in prison by the time I was twenty-one.

We finish our lunch without further drama and I return to the safety of my bed at the Y. This has certainly been some birthday weekend. I am so exhausted that I'm looking forward to Kalighat and the relative peace of routine.

 Returning to Kalighat on Monday after my short but sensational 'holiday', I feel like a whole new person. I am all sweetness and light; nothing and nobody can dent my feeling of goodwill.

Leaving work that night I soon discover that there are no buses, taxis or any other form of transport moving down A. M. Road. This is the main thoroughfare leading back to Chowringhee. I rarely read a newspaper and am seldom aware of what is happening in the city. I'm content to be surprised every time I encounter something new. We are in the middle of the Kali *puja*, the festival celebrating the goddess, and each evening the entire city celebrates with processions and fireworks. Needless to say, everything else grinds to a halt.

It is a beautiful evening. The road has been decorated with lights and for once I can walk unimpeded down the street. Lost in my own dreamland, I suddenly feel an almighty blow on my right hip and the next thing I know I am tossed into the air, landing on my left shoulder and my head. Raising my eyes I see the receding tail-lights of a car. The inevitable crowd of Indians are all jabbering and performing re-enactments of the collision. My white skin is for once a hindrance; everyone seems frightened to come near me or become involved. I spy my bag about 20 metres down the road and quickly realise that if I don't claim it swiftly I will lose it forever. My hands and knees propel me the required distance, and as I retrieve my bag I perform a quick assessment of my injuries. We in the medical profession always tend to apply the worst-case scenario to any diagnosis of our own injuries or ailments. As a result I decide on fractured skull, shoulder and hip.

Sitting in the middle of the street I am still confronted with the problem of transport. Although the people around me have shown concern, the only way to get home is to walk. Dragging myself into the upright position I find that my limbs still operate, if somewhat painfully. Progress is slow and with every step my sunny mood gives way to increasing anger. Obviously the car meant to hit me, as it had the entire road to itself. That I received only a glancing blow was more likely good luck than good management. My anger boils when I reflect on my numerous forays into the usually dense traffic, only to now be side-swiped by a lone idiot on an almost empty street. All nine million Indians in Calcutta are swept into the same bucket of condemnation as I stagger down the road.

The accuracy of my diagnosis can now be tested as I near the hallowed halls of the P.G. Hospital. Standing in front of this establishment I soon decide that my injuries are not as severe as I first thought; I would need to be at death's door and unconscious to allow myself to be treated here. By the time I finally turn the corner into Park Street, I'm floating along in a sea of self-pity, daring anyone to look sideways at me. This has been one of the longest nights in history and as I reach No. 18, my bed is all I can think of.

A stranger might describe the volunteer community of the Y as a caring and thoughtful lot, but he would be wrong.

Searching for some paracetamol leads me to another girl's room. When I ask if she has any headache tablets she replies with a laugh, 'What's wrong with you? It's a bit early for a hangover, isn't it?'

When I reply that I've just been run over by a car, she laughs hysterically. 'That's a good one,' she says.

I turn my back to walk away.

'Oh!' she suddenly exclaims. 'You really have been run over.'

'What changed your mind?' I demand.

'The skid marks up your back,' she merrily replies. I could happily kill her if only I were feeling a little stronger.

Once I have showered and reassessed my injuries, the toll is not all that terrible. I have lost a good deal of skin from my shoulder where I landed on the road but, apart from a large egg on my head, this is the only visible sign of my near-death experience. The major casualty of the night seems to be my bag. The shoulder strap snapped on impact when it was flung away, but the real and lasting damage is inside. Smashed to smithereens is my one and only jar of Vegemite. The pungent black food of life is smeared throughout the bag. An old set of plastic rosary beads has suffered an amputation of the crucifix and even they are now coated in Vegemite. I can live without the rosary beads but the destruction of the Vegemite is beyond the pale.

I hole up at No. 18 for the next few days and it is with major embarrassment that I greet Sister Luke and Sister Berchmans when they visit this poor victim of road carnage. They seem as disappointed as I that I can't produce more visible and dramatic injuries. I explain at great length the utter catastrophe of the Vegemite jar, but this does not make a major impression on them. They of course are beside themselves with jubilation when they find out I was carrying rosary beads in my bag. I can see Luke's mind working overtime on claiming me for the convent yet.

My recuperation lasts only a couple more days and then life returns to normal. And on my first day back I find that God is definitely in tune with Kalighat.

It seems that whenever the sisters require help, a quick prayer to the man upstairs is all it takes. It was during the monsoon season that I first experienced this phenomenon. It was pouring with rain and we had run out of clean sheets. I approached Sister Luke and asked her to unlock the extra linen cupboard. This request was treated as blasphemy. It was breaking that good old charge sister tradition of always guarding your secret linen supply for a real emergency. The problem with this tradition is that the sister in charge is the only interpreter of emergency. I received yet another clip around the head and was told, 'God's not stupid man. He knows the washing needs to dry.' Within minutes of this pronouncement

The indomitable duo: Sister Luke *(left)* and Sister Berchmans

the sun duly made an appearance, conveniently drying the washing. It took me several cigarettes to convince myself that it was all just a coincidence.

Today, however, I'm prepared to give it a shot. I only hope that God is as receptive to volunteers' requests as he is to those of the sisters. I've just spotted yet another group of tourists coming through the Kalighat doors. I recognise the Australian accent and race off quickly to find Sister Luke. She normally hides whenever the tourists appear, polite small talk not being her long suit. I implore her to go and be nice and to ask them for any Vegemite they might have. My suggestion is to say that it is of great benefit to the patients. All Australians know how healthy it is. Sister Luke plays her part to perfection and I even offer up a silent prayer when I see two ladies reach for their handbags. The only price I have to pay for these little jars of black gold is to attend adoration at the Mother House tonight. Sister Luke continues to measure me up for the blue-bordered sari.

This birthday week has turned out to be something of a roller-coaster ride. I was certainly on the up-slope on Friday and Saturday, suffering the first downer on Sunday when I nearly choked to death, only to recover and continue the ride. Monday brought me crashing back to earth only to rise once again on the wings of faith and Vegemite. I often wonder if this is all a dream and, if not, what it will be like to live in the real world again after this experience.

 Sister Luke and all at Kalighat are in a frenzy yet again. The cause of the mayhem this time is the annual street children's picnic. As far as I can ascertain, this event requires weeks of planning and preparation. The sisters entertain about 400 children from the general Kalighat area. During the past several days the lady on the sewing machine has been busily making a few hundred dresses in various sizes, while Sister Berchmans has been active in the markets, and hundreds of shirts and shorts are now vying for space in the linen cupboards. I have no clue as to the purpose of the new clothes and have discovered that any questions asked at this time are met with a manic scream from Sister Luke and the inevitable clip around the head.

I take refuge with the patients and continue the normal running of the home. The sisters have become totally fixated by the picnic preparations and we volunteers are left to the daily work of patient care. In the open plan of Kalighat, these preparations can be observed from a safe distance. The patients quickly adapt to the change in focus and, as masters in self-preservation, they make very few demands, accepting their meals and medication in an unusually subdued manner when the harried volunteers finally get to them. In a remarkable spirit of partnership, the volunteers and patients try to make it through each day without attracting attention from an increasingly agitated Sister Luke. I consider it another one of those little 'God things' that there are no catastrophes, such as lost bodies, poisoned patients, major fits or medical emergencies. Fear is a wonderful incentive. The most remarkable effect is that nobody has died in this last hectic week. We are all intrigued by the preparations and everyone waits to see the culmination of all this hysterical activity. Tomorrow is the big day and all volunteers and sisters are told to report bright and early.

Seven a.m. sees me wandering down Kalighat Road still half asleep. I am soon violently awakened when a veritable sea of children swarm upon me as I try to reach Kalighat's front door. There are hundreds and hundreds of children clamouring for attention and a place in the picnic. Small bodies have attached themselves to my legs and back, while several others try to dislocate my arms. I am rescued by a large Indian policeman brandishing a large wooden baton. He obviously enjoys his work and lays into my escorts with relish. Safely inside Kalighat, I retreat to the roof for a calming cigarette and survey the several hundred children massed below me. My intuition is predicting a disaster in the making.

Back downstairs in the hub of Kalighat, Sister Luke is organising the battle plans. Four hundred children will be allowed inside and these will be bathed and given new clothes. Part two of the exercise is to board buses and drive to the picnic area. Once the instructions have been given, we all man our posts. I have the dubious honour of front door selection duty. The customary method of selection seems to be the ability to pass between two arbitrary marks made on the door frame. The lower of these marks is around 75 centimetres and the higher is about 120 centimetres. There are well over 700 children facing us, all determined to be among the picnickers. The policeman on duty begins flourishing his baton as the crowd surges forward. I am reminded of rural Australia, as the front door is used in a similar fashion to a gate when drafting sheep. The passing smell of our young livestock is not all that dissimilar either. Several older children try to gain admission but the height rules are ferociously enforced by the brother on the door. I get sucked in by an older boy carrying a young cripple, only to see him drop his load instantly once in the door. I would throw him out if I could ever find him again in this pool of madness. I am an easy touch for the blind, lame and under-sized, who sense my vulnerability. Within half an hour the quota has been reached. A sister yells 'Enough' and the doors are locked shut.

The scene inside Kalighat resembles a plague of locusts descending on the patients. Little bodies are perched wherever they can find space. The wash area is a frenzy of activity as old, filthy clothes are discarded and small brown bodies are soaped, scrubbed and rinsed. These bedraggled figures are then passed down the line to be powdered and dressed in their smart new clothes. It is all a bit Cinderella-ish. Waifs of the streets go in one door and sweet little angels appear out the other side. The speed of the transformation is mind-numbing. As in all things, the children, sisters and workers take everything in their stride. It is only the poor bemused volunteers that flounder in the absurdity of the situation, trying to discover the rationale behind this dramatic transformation.

Once all the little urchins have been transformed, the boys' hair is oiled and combed while the girls' is plaited and tied with ribbons. God, they all look so sweet and innocent. Stage two of this exercise is to escort fifty children at a time onto each bus. In their new pristine state there is no chance of any interloper joining the group. One or two volunteers and a couple of sisters join each bus. As I board ours, I notice several empty 20-litre drums strategically placed up the aisle. The purpose of these containers is a mystery.

By 10.00 a.m. we are on the road and still in the dark as to our destination. The use of the biscuit tins becomes painfully obvious within fifteen minutes of travel. Excitement and the novelty of bus travel combine to produce a potent display of vomiting. We are kept busy while several children relieve themselves of whatever they last had to eat. In another piece of outstanding logic, we are trapped in the sweltering buses as they make their way through the centre of Calcutta all the way to the other side of the city. Kalighat is only minutes from Tollygunge and some lovely rural settings. Why we are travelling for two miserable hours in the opposite direction is quite beyond me.

Our destination proves to be the grounds of one of the Catholic schools. With undisguised relief the children make a hasty exit from the bus.

The food for today has been donated by local people and some businesses. Large tables have been erected and are laden with sweets and pastries. The children have their minds set on one thing only—to eat as much as possible. Another exercise in military planning has the children in single file marching past each of the different tables and collecting their food. They then form small groups and sit on the rather barren and dusty sports field to consume this remarkable feast. The richness and amount of food consumed is no doubt confounding the capacities of many a small belly. As soon as all the food and drink is either eaten or hidden the children start returning to their buses. Even the enthusiastic cajoling of some of the volunteers cannot persuade these children to participate in any games. It seems that their one and only purpose has been achieved and the idea of fun and games is secondary to a quick return to their familiar environment. Very few of the children speak English and most are too shy to have anything to do with us foreigners.

This remarkable picnic is over and we are back on the buses by 1.30 p.m., rolling back into the traffic. I work overtime on biscuit bucket duty, not always reaching my target in time. Several little explosions fail to miss me as a target. The traffic is even more congested on the return journey and it is close to 4.00 p.m. when the Kali Temple comes into view. There is no more welcome sight in all the world. Within moments of stopping, the children have disappeared, the only evidence of the day's activity the technicolour interior of the buses. A dozen smelly and bedraggled volunteers emerge like survivors of a bomb blast and we make our way into the relative sanity of Kalighat. Conversation is kept to a minimum and, after an essential wash, we feed and clean the patients before returning home.

As the afternoon draws to a close, we try to work out if today's picnic was a success. There is no general consensus and many different views on the definition of success in this context. I have no idea if the children enjoyed the day or not. Our Western perceptions are once again totally useless and irrelevant. As we collect our bags and prepare to leave Kalighat, Sister Luke thanks us all for our work, smiling from ear to ear. This to me is the only real indication we will have that today's expedition has actually been a triumph. A cigarette and several cold beers have never looked so inviting!

FIFTEEN

 Tonight Catherine and I are going down the road to the local Chinese restaurant for dinner. It is named the Waldorf, which gives me a giggle whenever I eat here. The food is wonderful, plentiful and fits within my budget. During the meal Catherine moans constantly about her love-life. She has met a Tanzanian man, Julius, at the Y and begun a romance with him. He is studying engineering at a college in Ranchi in the neighbouring state of Bihar. His absence is making her heart grow fonder and, as far as I'm concerned, her head grow weaker. It is definitely an obsession.

There are times in life when you should learn to keep your mouth shut; unfortunately, I have never learnt this lesson. By the time we finish our meal I am sick of hearing the name Julius. In my usual abrupt manner I ask, 'If you're so keen on this guy, why don't you just go and visit him?'

Catherine asks, 'Will you come with me?'

'Of course,' I reply, never dreaming she would actually go.

Within minutes she has paid for dinner and we are wending our way up Park Street. I have no idea where we are headed. Ten minutes later Catherine is searching the bus depot for a bus to Ranchi. My jaw nearly hits the ground when she returns with two tickets and informs me she has bought seats on the bus departing immediately.

To say we have seats is somewhat misleading. The only space available for us at this late stage is in the cabin of the bus itself. Climbing into the cabin I find my designated spot is the front dashboard, flush against the windscreen. While this position offers very scenic views, the 20-centimetre width of the dashboard provides limited support for my posterior. Catherine is perched on a plank running from the dashboard towards the back of the cabin. She has the window at her back but, alas, it has no glass. One wrong move and she is history.

The interior of the cabin displays all the usual Indian decorations. There are several photographs of the numerous gods and goddesses with a small shrine, complete with incense and flowers, behind the driver's seat. The cabin 'crew' comprises the driver, two men perched on boxes behind him, two more on the passenger seat and the largest Indian man I have ever seen lounging on the cowling covering the engine. This brings our total number to eight and provides very cramped quarters to say the least. Our companions are thrilled by the novelty of our presence and spend countless minutes leering in our direction. The large man seems to be in charge and introduces himself as 'Happy'. He is the only English-speaker and has a fairly limited vocabulary. His name is self-evident as he regales us with jokes and stories that only he can understand, his large body shaking the whole cabin at the end of each punchline. We politely join in the laughter.

The traffic of Calcutta is frightening at the best of times, but my position offers me a whole new perspective on the many close calls and potential disasters that are part and parcel of driving in this madhouse. I feel like a rabbit that has been caught in the headlights and is just waiting to be run over. I flinch every time we approach another vehicle or brake suddenly. This is definitely no time for sobriety. Unfortunately the lack of planning in this venture means I will be pinned in this position for the next thirteen hours. When will I ever learn to keep my mouth shut and steer clear of others' personal problems?

Hours creep by and Happy has had us all singing songs and telling stories. I have done my rendition of 'Waltzing Matilda', while Catherine graced us with 'Pack Up Your Troubles', which I thought was rather appropriate. In the early hours of the morning our companions are snoring complacently and the driver seems inclined to join them. My precarious position gives me ample room to judge his intermittent control of the steering wheel. As we drive directly towards several prone bodies asleep near the roadside, I yell loudly enough to wake not only the cabin occupants, including the driver, but all the other passengers on board. I am not popular.

By the grace of God, the gods and goddesses, karma or fate we arrive safely in Ranchi at 10.30 next morning. Climbing from the cabin, Catherine is unable to stand erect following her enforced forward crouch of the past thirteen hours. My left buttock and leg are in a state of paralysis and my hands are in a permanently splayed position from trying to grip the windscreen. God, I hope this fellow is worth it!

After completing a series of stretching manoeuvres, Catherine and I are once again fit to rejoin the human race. She has now discovered that her beloved's college is situated about 15 kilometres out of town and the only available transport is a three-wheeled mini taxi. Three-quarters of an hour later we emerge from an experience that can only be likened to the bone-jarring action of a tumble dryer. Julius is found and the young lovers are ecstatic. I reach for yet another cigarette and wish I was back at Kalighat.

Within half an hour we are on the road again and heading back to Ranchi. A hotel is found, rooms booked and movement for the moment is halted. I have nothing with me: no clothes, no toothbrush, no soap or towel and certainly no sense of humour. Julius makes a hasty trip to purchase a few essentials, after which I take a refreshing shower and lie down in peace and quiet.

Food is the next item on the agenda and we eventually find ourselves at a place called the 'Have More Restaurant'. This fine establishment has over one hundred items listed in its menu. With my hunger pangs growing, I order No. 23, No. 37 and No. 86.

The waiter gives me the universal sad Indian look. 'Oh! So sorry mem-sahib, we not have that today.'

Further enquiries uncover the fact that only No. 6 (a mutton curry) is available. My day is certainly not getting any better. I have a quick meal, leaving the others to linger over coffee, and return to my bed before my exasperation can get the better of me. Julius and Catherine are floating along in their own little world.

That night we go out to a restaurant and nightclub. Mike, another Tanzanian man, has joined us for the evening. I met him several weeks ago when all the students were staying at the Y. It quickly dawns on me that he thinks I too have travelled all this way just to see him. Unfortunately for him my attitude towards romance has taken a considerable nosedive in the last twenty-four hours and I deal with him in a rather frank and brutal manner. Despite my partner's obvious dejection, the evening is quite pleasant and I consume enough alcohol to calm my frustration and actually enjoy myself.

The next day finds Catherine and I once again boarding a bus. Thankfully, this time we sit on real seats. The glow on Catherine's face and the emotional farewell to Julius indicate that the trip has been an outstanding success. I even feel a little pride in my part of the experience. But these feelings of goodwill evaporate with each passing hour and the rising temperature. Perspiration soaks my already putrid clothes and their offensive smell is only masked by the odour of the assorted livestock travelling aboard this bone rattler.

I swear to myself and to Catherine that I will never offer personal advice or help. My days as an agony aunt are over. Amazing as it may seem, I can't wait to see the smog and congestion of Calcutta. I won't be happy until I'm striding down Park Street and rounding the corner for the Y. The really scary thought to emerge from the last forty-eight hours is that Kalighat now seems relatively safe and sane. I must be losing my grip!

 Margaret is an old school friend from Toowoomba. She has been travelling around India and has finally settled in Calcutta. Having visited several of Mother Teresa's homes and various other organisations in Calcutta she decided to live and work with a L'Arche community here. These are run under the auspices of Jean Vanier and consist of homes for the mentally handicapped. I don't know if I would be able to live in her shoes but she is very happy and enjoys the work. As in all things, life in her community has its humorous moments. Every time I visit I manage to lose all my cigarettes to a host of charming but manic residents.

As Margaret only has Wednesdays off we meet at the Y each week for Vegemite Wednesdays. I am the repository of all known Vegemite supplies in Calcutta. It is a delicacy only another Australian can really appreciate which fortunately reduces the competition for this luxury item. When I return from the morning session at Kalighat, Margaret and I make our way to the GPO to retrieve our mail. Mail to us is like a blood transfusion to a haemophiliac. The injection of news from home always manages to revive a waning spirit; it reminds us what normal really means. Margaret and I are lucky in that we can share family news as we both know each other's family and have many friends in common. This is a particular bonus when one of us is facing an empty box. The most gut-wrenching sight of all is facing two empty boxes. On these occasions we bad-mouth every member of our combined families plus every friend and acquaintance we can think of on the journey back to the Y.

It is the return journey from the GPO that lends its name to Vegemite Wednesdays. We hit every coffee shop selling hot buttered toast and munch our way back to the Y. Needless to say the Vegemite attracts many comments and offensive remarks from the numerous waiters and interested observers.

This particular day we are both recipients of massive mail. With Christmas approaching our families have obviously decided to get in early. My mother is my most consistent and faithful correspondent and this time has outdone herself with a post-bag full of goodies. The ever-vigilant bureaucracy of the Indian Postal Service requires several forms to be signed in order to receive a parcel. On this occasion, receipt of my parcel requires two hours, several cigarettes and a few rupees. Margaret and I have both been in India long enough now to accept these delays in the relatively sure knowledge that we will eventually receive the parcel.

We rush to our first Vegemite stop, eager to open our mail. My very valuable post-bag contains a bottle of lice shampoo, some scabies cream, a nit comb, a container of Vegemite, two rolls of film and an audio cassette marked 'Merry Christmas'. My mother is nothing if not practical! Once we stop laughing at the selection of goods I do manage to acknowledge their usefulness. Margaret has received many cards and letters and our Vegemite stops are rather extended as we make our way home.

As I do not possess a tape player, I have to ask Therese, an American volunteer, for the loan of hers. She feels a proprietorial responsibility, so she and Patty join Margaret and I in my room to listen to the tape. My brother Richard has orchestrated its making and, as he is somewhat prone to theatrics, I know I am bound to be embarrassed. The opening number is Peter Allen singing 'I Still Call Australia Home'. This is followed by Richard explaining the reasons for the tape and difficulties involved. As he is studying for the priesthood at the Banyo Seminary one could say that he has been bitten by the religious bug and, much to my horror, he goes right over the top in some of his comments. He waffles on and on, expressing his admiration for the work I am doing and trying to give it some theological basis. This reduces Therese and Patty to tears and Margaret and I to fits of laughter. Several other volunteers are also listening in, as the three-quarter height walls provide wonderful acoustics. Their tears, laughter and other responses can also be heard. Numerous other relatives' and friends' voices emanate from this small machine and when a group of them give a rendition of 'Waltzing Matilda' accompanied by the spoons, Margaret and I are nearly apoplectic and the rest of the Y is awash with tears. Richard follows this up with an emotional monologue on service and caring—'Bridge Over Troubled Waters' playing in the background. By this time the entire first floor is sobbing madly. My mother finishes the tape off and when she signs off, 'Your mother . . . Joan' everyone starts cheering!

I love my family dearly, but this has been a most embarrassing experience. While I wallow in self-pity other voices are calling out for a replay. I don't think I've had a private moment since I came to this bloody country. We play it again and I finally relax and enjoy the good wishes. Margaret and I continue to laugh as we recognise different voices, envisaging the party occasioned by the making of this tape and wishing we had been there.

My tape has become communal property, but no-one else seems interested in my more practical gifts.

SEVENTEEN

Christmas is here already. I can't believe how fast the time has flown. Even in a predominantly Hindu country such as this, the trappings of the Christmas season can be found. A large tree has been decorated outside the Park Hotel and most shops and businesses display some form of decoration. The ever-present public loudspeakers now pound out old Christmas carols instead of the steady diet of ear-piercing Indian music. After a week of this I'm not sure which is worse.

All the volunteers are going to the Mother House tonight for midnight mass. As we make our way upstairs to the chapel, Sister Luke catches my eye and gives me one of those triumphant smiles as if to say, 'We've got you this time!' The chapel is a large bare room save for a modest altar, tabernacle, crucifix and stations of the Cross. It is filled tonight with 400 sisters all kneeling or sitting on the floor. Volunteers and other outsiders are directed to the rear of the right-hand side. Mother Teresa is in attendance tonight, barely discernible as a small humped figure kneeling near the back wall, directly facing the tabernacle. Mass gets underway and there is a wonderful feeling of joy and life all around. The enthusiasm and spirit of the sisters is infectious. But when the mass has ended, my spiritual flight is suddenly brought back to earth when the choir of hundreds of Indian voices sings, 'Happy Birthday to Jesus'. I fall about the place laughing yet again at the craziness of Calcutta. We volunteers sing 'Happy Birthday to Jesus' all the way home, much to the dismay of the dozens of sleeping bodies we step over.

*

Christmas Day at Kalighat is much the same as any other day. The patients have to be washed and medications given. The mood is more festive and the sisters have prepared a Christmas lunch for the volunteers. When the work is over we all gather around a large table and ready ourselves for a feast. Sister Luke has spent all morning preparing this food; it is her only way of expressing thanks and appreciation for the work of the volunteers. Platters of fried chicken and fried rice are brought out and special plastic plates are provided to each volunteer. The usual tin plates used for the patients have obviously been deemed unworthy. With our chicken and rice and glasses of cordial we celebrate the Christmas of 1981. Sister Luke presses more food upon me as I polish off the contents of my plate. I thank her profusely, but try to make a quiet exit as twelve midday has come and gone and I have another appointment at one o'clock.

I make it back to the Y just in time to round up a few of the girls and be ready for Norman to pick us up. He has graciously volunteered to host a Christmas lunch for me and any of the other girls who have nowhere to go. Once at Norman's place we waste no time in devouring his ample supply of liquor. Christmas carols are played at full volume and within the hour everyone is suitably merry and in fine voice. Norman's houseboy/cook has outdone himself this time. With six of us seated around the table he makes a triumphant entrance with a large roast turkey, followed by a baked ham, roast potatoes and pumpkin, cauliflower in white sauce, peas and broccoli. The poor fellow nearly dies of embarrassment as we stand and applaud him and a couple of the girls propose marriage. We wait an appropriate minute or two, then fall upon this feast with gusto. There is no more appreciative diner than a volunteer living in a foreign country and presented with a traditional Western Christmas dinner. Food is a volunteer's main obsession.

Following lunch we relax with a few more drinks and tell tales of Christmases past. I glance at my watch and realise that I am late for another engagement. Reluctantly leaving Norman and the girls, I grab a cab to the home of Mr Sherman, the US Consul General. I'm not quite sure how I came to make my Christmas Day arrangements and it was only that morning that I realised I was somewhat overbooked. I can't now remember how I managed to be invited to the Consul General's. No doubt alcohol was involved.

Arriving at the Shermans' residence, I pass through the security gates and make a fashionably late entrance. Therese and Patty are already here, as are about twenty or more other guests. I feel a little self-conscious about my attire as it is the same cotton trousers, T-shirt and thongs that I wore to Kalighat this morning. Shrugging my shoulders, I accept yet another drink from a passing waiter and start to mingle with the guests. My stomach gives a loud groan as I glance at the table laden with crockery, cutlery and glassware in the dining room. Patty tells me that Christmas lunch will be served shortly. I don't know if my digestive tract will ever forgive me.

The full services of the consular staff have produced an outstanding meal and I am halfway through the main course of turkey with all the trimmings before I finally twig that there is something different about this group. Many of the guests burst into fits of laughter when they realise that I have only just figured out that they are deaf! My over-extended stomach is now tied in knots. I am rarely lost for words but this time I've really stepped in it!

It transpires that they are an American travelling theatre group called Theatre of the Deaf. Everyone gets much enjoyment out of my discomfort and I try to brazen my way out by saying that I'm a very non-discriminatory person and had assumed that they were just very good listeners. This rather improbable explanation brings on more hilarity and I am nearly the cause of more disaster as several guests choke on their desserts. I down a few more calming drinks, vaguely wondering if my alcohol consumption might be contributing to this mayhem. But by this stage I am past caring and continue to chat with the deaf contingent after lunch. They even provide me with free tickets to their performances.

As the evening draws on, Therese, Patty and I are the last of the guests. As Mr and Mrs Sherman have to leave for another engagement they invite us to stay on with their son Justin. We watch videos and talk for a while and the events of the day start to catch up with me. Mrs Sherman has also invited us to stay the night and I will never say no to hot water and air-conditioning. A shower is a little beyond my capabilities tonight, but as I draw back the bedcovers the sparkling white sheets hurt my eyes. One look at my black, dirt-encrusted feet causes me great shame and regret. My befuddled answer to this dilemma is to remove the sheets and climb onto the bare mattress. Pride and comfort satisfied in one blow.

The next morning I luxuriate in a lovely hot bath and reflect on the previous day's events. Overall I think I managed my three Christmas lunches quite well, though the mere thought of another turkey does horrible things to my stomach. As I join Mrs Sherman and the girls for coffee, they diplomatically refrain from bringing up too many of my *faux pas* from yesterday, except to enquire into my hearing.

EIGHTEEN

 Calcutta screams at you, pulls at you and overwhelms you. Nine million people are squeezed into an area smaller than the size of Brisbane. The noise is deafening. Hawkers screaming in the streets, the continual and insistent honking of horns and the incessant music blaring through loudspeakers combine to create a cacophony that would rival the decibel levels of most rock bands. This auditory assault is matched and even surpassed by the levels of pollution. A black pall hangs over the city, a combination of vehicle exhaust, smoke from cooking fires—which use a unique fuel combination of cow manure and coal dust—and toxic emissions from various industrial stacks. This oppressive weight produces a greenhouse effect on all below it, exacerbating the noise, heat and humidity.

The difficulties of living in Calcutta are starting to take their toll on me. I am becoming obsessed with the pollution and long for the day when I will be able to blow my nose and not be greeted with a disgusting black mess in my tissue. This atmospheric debris not only infests my respiratory system but manages to coat and clog every exposed pore of my skin. I have given up all hope of ever having clean feet again until I am back in pristine Toowoomba.

My most constant longing is for an automatic washing machine or my mother—whichever I find first. Most of the girls here use the magical services of the dhobi, the Indian name for the laundry man. You drop your dirty washing at his feet in the morning and by that evening it is returned washed, ironed and folded. His services are extremely cheap by Western standards, but my limited finances have caused me to economise in all matters but cigarettes and alcohol. My alternative to the dhobi is to collect all my filthy clothes once a week and, together with a plastic bucket and a trusty bar of blue washing soap, perform my interpretation of the Indian washing method. First I fill the plastic bucket with water as insurance against the tap suddenly ceasing to flow. Then I soak all my clothes in the shower, introduce them to the soap, and proceed to bash hell out of them on the concrete floor. It doesn't really get my clothes clean but it relieves a lot of tension. After this violent episode, a quick rinse and a wring and these garments are once again ready to adorn the wires running across my room. I have never enjoyed housework!

I am physically, emotionally and financially exhausted. I have survived nine months here and now is the time to return home. But once I have made the decision and booked my flight, I'm assailed by doubts and insecurities. In a few short weeks I will be back in Toowoomba and it will be as if none of this has ever happened. Fortunately for my sanity's sake, lack of funds dictates my imminent departure.

Calcutta can have a very detrimental effect on some people and during my time here I've seen several volunteers come with high expectations, only to suffer an emotional breakdown. The never-ending supply of the destitute to fill the Kalighat beds and the inevitable fate of all these people leaves me desperate to apportion blame and stop the deadly cycle. My frustration levels have been steadily rising over the past few months and I've begun to think that the next home I find might be jail if I don't leave first. From the beginning I have had a somewhat violent response to the maze of inconsistencies that govern daily life here. I have mainly resorted to verbal jousting, although on occasion I have gained great satisfaction from a blow well delivered on the buses. Oddly enough, now that I have decided to return home I'm no longer frustrated and have become happily impervious to the mayhem.

*

Sister Luke has decided that I must meet Mother Teresa before I leave. To be perfectly frank, it doesn't worry me one way or the other. It was because of her name and notoriety that I first came to Calcutta but I have discovered that it is the patients and the work that are the more important to me. Mother is like a magnet that draws people in and many come just because of her fame. I've been at the Mother House and seen dozens of foreigners surround her, waiting to get her autograph. She obliges all these people and dispenses blessings and words of comfort, yet I can't help but feel sorry for the poor old lady and wish that they'd just leave her in peace. This is the price of fame and she is treated in much the same way as any famous star.

The price of this type of fame extends to all the homes, and it is not unusual for groups of tourists to come to have a look. Awareness of the plight of the poor is one thing but the voyeuristic attitude of a lot of these tourists makes my blood boil. When they descend on Kalighat and wander around the wards with shocked expressions and handkerchiefs clasped to their mouths, the dignity of the patients is invaded. I have had to physically restrain some tourists from taking photographs. They ask permission neither of the sisters nor the patients, and this gross insult is one of the many negatives of Mother Teresa's fame.

The other group that regularly invades the homes in Calcutta is the documentary film-makers. As always with human beings, there are the good and the bad. The humorous side to these events is that film-going is the most important pastime in India, so when the patients see the lights and cameras, they mistakenly believe they too are headed for the big screen. Only the seriously ill have no interest in these happenings and of course these are the only ones that make it onto the film. There was one director, however, who indulged all the patients in their thespian aspirations, and he did more for their wellbeing than we ever could.

Today as I enter Kalighat, Sister Luke is having yet another manic episode. She eagerly informs me that Mother T is coming for a visit. As any nurse will know, the imminent arrival of the matron can send many charge sisters into previously unimagined paroxysms of cleanliness and patient preparation. Only when Sister Luke finally has all of us reduced to emotional and physical exhaustion does she stop shouting.

Mother Teresa starts the visit with a prayer to Mary, and then she seems to ignore her surroundings and Sister Luke, spending her time talking to the patients. It is during this time that I realise to what extent the trappings of fame and expansion have denied her the real joy that only working with these people can give. A day of anonymous feeding and cleaning would be for her a golden dream. She certainly has a presence;

Mother Teresa on a visit to Kalighat

each and every one of the patients seems to find some comfort from the time she spends with them.

Sister Luke finally grabs me by the arm and introduces me to Mother. She offers me a blue-bordered sari. I tell her that they don't make them in my size, and that is the end of the conversation, much to Sister Luke's annoyance. I, on the other hand, can well understand Mother T's preference for the patients and am simply grateful that I have witnessed her devotion here.

As fate would have it, my mother met Mother Teresa before I did. Mother T visited Australia and opened the new Mater Mothers' Hospital; as my mother is a past nurse there, she attended the opening. She met Mother Teresa and told her that I was working in Calcutta. Mother nodded and said, 'Oh, yes, I know her'. It certainly made my mother feel better even if it wasn't the truth. Even living saints tell the occasional white lie!

 Walking down Kalighat Road for the last time makes me more aware than ever of the life and vitality that exists here. Everything is exaggerated, colours seem more startling, sounds are more acute, the perennial rhythm of the city conceals its frequent life-changing experiences. I have wandered down this street hundreds of times as part of the great Calcuttan mass, only vaguely aware of my surroundings. Now the thought of not being part of this experience causes an incredible sense of loss. I have to remind myself how much I hate the filth, noise and the crowds. The mind is a very fragile mechanism and I am obviously getting out in the nick of time.

Leaving Kalighat this last night is the most gut-wrenching experience of my life. I try to spend the day normally but the thought of so many 'last' experiences is overwhelming. The roof and my cigarettes are working overtime! I say a last goodbye to each of the patients and staff and step up onto the platform at the end of the male ward to retrieve my bag from on top of the cupboard. Sister Luke finally emerges from wherever she has been hiding all day and we face each other as two of the most undemonstrative human

beings on earth. I'm sure that's part of the reason we
have got along together so well. I thank her for allowing me to work here and for all she has taught me
and she reciprocates by telling me that it is all God's
work and not to forget about mass. Once a nun always
a nun! After this moving farewell it is a quick exit from
the door and down the steps.

As I scramble in my bag for a relieving cigarette,
my vision blurs and tears fall down my face. With shaking hands I finally manage to light a smoke, dry my
eyes and then shake my head in wonder at the effect
Kalighat has had on me over these past nine months.
It has been both the longest and briefest period in my
life. I know that a big part of me will always remain
at Kalighat. Sitting on the bus I reflect on the changes
in me and all the things that I have witnessed and
experienced. I wonder if they show, and what my
family and friends will think when I return home.
Calcutta and its people have slipped past my defences
and are now as much a part of my being as the dirt
in my feet—in fact the dirt will prove much easier to
eventually remove.

Another aeroplane, another seat and once again
I'm looking down on the roofs of Calcutta. I find it
hard to remember the dreams and aspirations of the
person I was when I first saw this city. My idealism has
been severely dented and reality has taught me many
harsh lessons about saving the world. I've also learnt
that Mother Teresa is not a superwoman but an ordinary one, doing ordinary things, and that there are
hundreds just like her all over Calcutta. I have
watched too many people die and have learnt to

accept and not fear death, but also to rail against the injustices that decree the poor should suffer the greatest burdens. I have experienced friendships that I hope will stay with me throughout my life. Above all I have learnt the value of humour and the importance of fun and joy in the lives of rich and poor alike.

The tourist book was right, Calcutta does assault the senses like no other city on earth. I have had senses assaulted that I never knew I possessed.

PART TWO

Second Chance
India, July 1983–December 1984

 Here I go again, sitting in my seat anxiously waiting to land on Indian soil once more. As an experienced traveller I am trying to appear very nonchalant as the plane approaches Madras Airport. My stomach, nonetheless, is tied in knots and my heart is racing. As I disembark and the Indian night aromas of smoke, incense, humidity and humanity envelop me, I have an overwhelming feeling of coming home. India claimed part of my being eighteen months ago and now I've returned to replenish my soul.

This time I'm ready for all contingencies. I'm armed with my own copy of the traveller's bible, *India, a Travel Survival Kit.* This essential publication gives all the information any traveller could need on accommodation, meals, transport, places of interest, history and culture all over India. My plan is to get to a place called Pondicherry as quickly as possible to meet up with a nun whom I got to know back in Australia. The first piece of business, though, is to clear customs here in Madras. Unfortunately one of the other foreigners has tried to bring in a large camera outfit without declaring it, so the rest of us white-skinned people are automatically under a cloud of suspicion. Along with two other Westerners I empty all my worldly possessions onto the floor and wait the obligatory two hours while the officials decide our fate. God, how I've missed Indian bureaucracy!

Finally the two lads and I collect our belongings and emerge into the Indian night, only to discover that all the taxis and rickshaws have left for the evening. As each of us is equipped with the bible we quickly work out the general direction in which we must head and make our way towards civilisation on foot. After several hours of walking we eventually stumble across a Salvation Army hostel and gladly book in for the night.

Madras is nothing like Calcutta. It is less crowded; the urgency is absent and pace of life much slower. The city is like a much younger sibling, learning new ways without the arrogance and superior airs of age. Not surprisingly, though, the more relaxed and carefree atmosphere only exacerbates the overwhelmingly inefficient bureaucracies. It takes two days of searching and questioning before I can finally obtain a bus ticket to Pondicherry. Happily, these small successes always fill a hapless foreigner with an inordinate sense of achievement.

Sitting in the bus, I once again question the wisdom of my actions. The last eighteen months in Toowoomba were fairly frustrating as I tried to settle back into an affluent Western culture. We take so many material things for granted in Australia that feelings of guilt and the excesses of this society left me feeling helpless. Only when I returned home did the enormous disparities between India and Australia strike me forcibly. At first I worshipped the automatic washing machine, marvelled at the wonders of continuous hot water and electricity, salivated over tender, juicy steaks, and wallowed with hedonistic pleasure in all the delights that Western society takes for granted—and felt guilty for doing so. Very quickly I found that I had ceased to appreciate the basics of everyday life. It is impossible to explain to others what everyday life in Calcutta is like, or to expect them to understand the enormous emotional and spiritual effect it has had on me.

As the months progressed, my memory dimmed and I once again became immersed in ordinary Australian life, my conscience giving me only infrequent kicks to try and shake my complacency. But frustration and a chance meeting with an Indian doctor ensured my return to India. As the gods would have it, this doctor just happened to be a sister in the Order of the Immaculate Heart in southern India. It seems that I'm destined to work with nuns.

Sister Gentiana told me about the work of her order, and as she described clinics, hospitals and work with the lepers, I felt a resurgence of enthusiasm to do something both useful and adventurous. Although Sister Gentiana was vague about what specific work I would do, she warmly encouraged me to journey to Pondicherry and offer my services. So here I am, again ready to step out into the unknown.

If it appears to you that I don't really know what I am doing here, then spare a thought for the poor Mother Superior in Pondicherry. I arrive unannounced on her doorstep, dirty and sweaty after a four-hour bus trip, wearing my customary outfit of cotton trousers, T-shirt and backpack, and offering to help with the work of her order. She has no idea of who or what I am. Sister Gentiana has neglected to inform her of my imminent arrival. However, the Mother Superior is most generous in offering me food and accommodation, and wanders away, shaking her head. Obviously the phenomenon of foreign volunteers descending on her order is a new and somewhat disconcerting one. I wonder how Mother Teresa's first volunteer felt? I sit forlornly in my room, trying to blow the cigarette smoke out the window, and questioning the wisdom of yet another of my rather rash and impulsive decisions.

During the following twenty-four hours the Mother Superior tries desperately to find somewhere else for me to go. A mission hospital in a place called Pulambaddy is deemed the most suitable and with an audible sigh of relief she entrusts me to the care of a young sister. Once again we board a bus.

My young companion can hardly understand English and I know nothing of the language spoken in this part of the country, which is Tamil. Each area in India has its own language and there seems to be very little compatibility between them. English is certainly not as widespread here in the south as in the north. We travel for six very quiet hours to a place called Trichy and there change buses for a further two-and-a-half-hour journey to Pulambaddy.

This turns out to be a small town with dusty unpaved streets, low buildings and a bustling market atmosphere. The largest and most substantial build-ings in the town lie behind the gates proclaiming the Sagaya Matha Hospital. This is our destination and, once inside, the hapless young sister is left to explain her most unusual companion to the sister in charge. All the sisters are dressed in formal long habits with accompanying severe head wear, much like nuns in Australia in the 1950s. I am left on my own with a cool drink while the sisters retire to decide my fate. I don't think the sister in charge is all that overjoyed at the prospect of having a foreign volunteer. It's at times like these that I thank God for the existence of a vow of obedience which precludes them from putting me on the next bus out of here. My triumphant return to India is not going as smoothly as I'd hoped.

 The verdict seems to be that I am to be given living quarters over the garage and once I've settled in a more definitive role can be found for me. My accommodation comprises two rooms, the first being something of a storeroom and the other a bright green room with a bed, table and chair. There is an attached wash stall with water tank and a separate Indian-style toilet. It is not exactly the Ritz but quite comfortable by Indian standards. Separated from the convent by a large open area, it is like being marooned on an island with no other people within sight nor sound.

My sense of isolation begins with the arrival of my evening meal. Two of the kitchen girls appear at the door brandishing a tiffin carrier (a stack of round metal containers used to carry food) and assorted crockery and cutlery. The girls can speak no English and, after several minutes of staring and giggling, they leave me to get on with my dinner. This meal is like many others in the south—hot and vegetarian with plenty of rice. While my culinary tastes have expanded somewhat over the last couple of years, a small amount of this food is enough for me. The girls return a short while later with, of all things, a glass of warm milk and retrieve my barely touched tiffin carrier. They open it to check the contents, gaze at me in horror and then fly off into rapid Tamil, leaving me feeling as if I have just murdered their entire families!

*

The pealing of the church bells wakens me at 5.30 in the morning. By some divine plan, my humble abode is adjacent to the church and the enthusiastic bell-ringing reverberates deafeningly around my room. After a quick wash, I join the sisters and staff for mass, which is in Tamil, of course. My dependable meal providers arrive with my breakfast, which consists of steamed rice patties called *idlys* and two different chutneys. Vegemite and *idlys* are not an obvious combination, but edible all the same. The rest of the day I spend waiting for one of the sisters to arrive and show me around the hospital but my only contact with the outside world is the kitchen girls and their never-ending meals. My decision to follow Sister Gentiana's advice is proving to be soul-destroying; the inactivity and isolation are enough to drive a body to drink. I have a bottle of duty-free rum in my bag and I'm sorely tempted to once again abandon my promise to turn over a new leaf.

The next morning after mass and breakfast Sister Fatima gives me a tour of the hospital. It is a well-run institution with medical, surgical and maternity wards. They also train their own nursing staff and have an attached leprosy unit with twenty inpatient beds. The entire place is clean and bright with a bustling atmosphere as the patients are brought in here from the surrounding villages. It seems painfully obvious to me that they do not require my services, but if I persevere here a little longer I may be able to learn something. I have always had an interest in leprosy and would dearly love to learn more about this horrendous disease but the sister in charge seems a little cool when we are introduced. I will have to step carefully.

During the next few days I make tentative forays onto the wards and create much excitement among patients and staff alike. I eventually find an English speaker in the resident doctor and spend a couple of hours each morning with him in the outpatients clinic. It is wonderful to speak and be understood and he helpfully explains the different diseases and conditions he is treating. He is a lovely old guy but spends a lot of time regaling me with stories of his university days and all the English books that he has read.

My only role here seems to be as a novelty item. At least the children appear to appreciate my presence and flock around me whenever I venture outdoors. The white-skinned, female foreigner has created quite an interest for the inhabitants of Pulambaddy.

My first foray beyond the convent and hospital was to attend a demonstration against the treatment of Tamils in Sri Lanka, although I had no idea what it was all about. I've joined Communist and Congress demonstrations in Calcutta before and always found them a great way of meeting people!

*

Two weeks since my arrival and I finally manage to attend the leprosy ward. The sister in charge is not quite the ogre I first thought. All I really know about lepers is what I have heard in the old Bible stories and a book I once read about Father Damien. These texts have a lot to answer for. Images of grossly disfigured people with oozing sores and ringing bells are quickly dispelled as I tour the inpatient section and meet the thirty or so longer-stay patients. Most long-term leprosy victims have a very pronounced facial characteristic which gives them a lion-like appearance. They have lost the cartilage in their eyebrows and nose and as a result their faces flatten out, thus resembling a lion. As for the oozing sores, these are treated like any other ulcer and each person has a very normal looking dressing and bandage. The only bells in evidence are the ones that disturb my sleep each morning. I had consciously prepared myself not to show any reluctance when touching these people. As I smilingly shake someone's badly deformed hand, I realise that this is about the fourth time I've done so—my mind is just catching up.

I spend the morning in the dressing room observing the treatment of the various ulcers. These outpatients are all chronic leprosy sufferers and, while they receive treatment to cure their disease, the long-term nerve damage is mainly responsible for the development of the ulcers. The only compensating factor for them is that the lack of sensation makes removing dead tissue and cleaning the ulcer virtually

painless. The only discordant note all morning is
when I try to bandage a man's foot with a bright
orange bandage. I am soon made aware that clinical
white is the preference of most patients as the
coloured bandages tend to mark the person out as
different. I'm happy to conform with their wishes and
give each bandaging my most professional attention,
thus earning Most Favoured Dresser status. At last I've
found a place where I can at least feel useful.

In the evening I attend my first operation here. It
is an emergency hernia. While the theatre is very
primitive, it has all the basic equipment. The real novelty of the whole enterprise is a power failure, obliging
us to work by candle- and torchlight. I love being in
India; any adversity is simply accepted with a shrug of
the shoulders and new/old ways are used to circum-
vent the obstacle, although how we managed not to
blow up the entire hospital with the candles and
oxygen still has me baffled.

My next foray is into the maternity wards and it is
with some trepidation that I witness my first delivery
here. The labour ward is equipped with two narrow
metal beds complete with metal stirrup supports and
a gleaming stainless steel bucket at the end of each
bed. The equipment for the newborn babies consists
of a rectangular metal tray, a rubber tube with manual
suction bulb, scissors and sterile tape for the umbili-
cal cord. Comfort is obviously not the major priority
in this labour ward. The preponderance of bare metal
will at least provide ease of cleaning and prevent cross
infection. As the delivery gets under way, I'm sure the
poor woman on the table wouldn't care if she was in

a five-star hospital with all the creature comforts; all she wants is to be rid of the pains screaming through her body. Suddenly a shock of black hair emerges, quickly followed by the rest of a slithering body. The baby is placed in the tray, then given a quick suction and clean before being placed in his mother's arms. The whole procedure is clean and competent; within thirty minutes both mother and baby are back in the main ward together, in the same bed. This is definitely

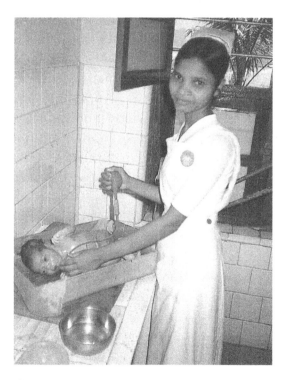

The maternity ward at Pulambaddy: a wonderful facility
for the surrounding villages but finding the transport to
get there was often a problem

my type of labour ward—no mucking about and no fuss or bother.

This birthing facility is a wonderful place for the village women to have available, but the lack of adequate transport is brought home to me later that same afternoon when a lady appears on the back of a bullock cart. She had started to give birth in her village and the baby's head had appeared. When the rest of the baby refused to move, her only option was to travel eight hours to reach help here. The baby had obviously died long before they reached the hospital but we were able to save the mother. Infant mortality is high in India but with places such as this little hospital, it can only improve.

By this time my dietary habits have occasioned a visit from the Sister Superior. Apparently my lack of appetite has them all worried and she has come to enquire if I am vegetarian or non-vegetarian. Upon hearing of my non-vegetarian status she proudly tells me that I will now receive an egg with breakfast. I'm sure this will help no end.

*

As the weeks go by, I establish a pattern of attending the mobile leprosy clinics three mornings a week and leprosy outpatients two mornings, while maintaining a presence each afternoon at maternity—an odd combination in anyone's thinking but this is India and all things are possible.

The mobile leprosy clinics provide by far the most interesting part of my day. We drive out each morning at 5.30 a.m. and visit several outlying villages where we distribute medication and do dressings. I love seeing the local village life and am very tempted to stay at one place when I discover the entire population gathered around a television set watching the test cricket. Once they discover that I am Australian they assume I know Dennis Lillee, and I say nothing to disabuse them. Cricket is a universal conversation point between ardent followers and our lack of common language proves no barrier. I am disappointed and reluctant to leave when the clinic van stops to pick me up at the end of its round.

On another particularly memorable village adventure I accompany a group of lepers to kill and butcher a cow. This whole group has hardly a working finger between them and the thought of them wielding axes and knives hardly bears thinking about. But necessity is said to be the mother of invention. Years of expertise have gone into fashioning a variety of instruments that can be attached to these mutilated limbs, and within minutes the beast is well and truly dismembered. After watching this performance, however, I am not sure that all their digits have been lost to the ravages of disease.

 Social life in Pulambaddy is non-existent. My daily outings to the leprosy clinic and maternity ward are the only real reprieve from my green room. Every time I set out on a new adventure I always tell myself that this time I'll be good and not succumb to my weakness for a few beers and a wild party. This time I don't even have the opportunity of token resistance. My mother would laugh herself silly if she could see me now; a more sober and demure citizen would be hard to find. I spend countless hours in my room contemplating the meaning of life and talking English to myself in a small mirror that I have found. This idea of turning over a new leaf is beginning to wear very thin.

My forays into the town of Pulambaddy take me as far as the post office and the bank. I'm a big hit in both of these establishments, as anyone with a dozen words of English tries to impress their workmates with their bilingual skills. Everyone in the post office knows exactly how many letters I have received and who has sent them. It's like having an extended family. The local bank has also attained higher status as a result of my visit. When I went to cash a $20 travellers cheque, consternation swept through the office. I was given a cup of tea and an English language newspaper while they tried to contact Trichy, the nearest 'large' town, to ascertain the correct procedure. My passport was passed around for everyone to marvel over and eventually I was asked to return the following day for my money. The banks in Calcutta were slow, but this far surpassed Calcutta's finest records. The following afternoon the manager greeted me with another cup of tea and handed over 200 rupees, all in two-rupee notes. The most remarkable aspect of this whole transaction was the small-denomination notes. I had always found it impossible to acquire small bills from any bank, so I considered the two-rupee notes a miraculous happening. The banks in the big cities will only give you large-denomination notes which none of the shopkeepers—or anyone else for that matter—are ever able to change. The status of the Pulambaddy branch had just been raised to cover international transactions and all members of the bank seemed to glow with pride.

The big event on the local social calendar is the screening of a Tamil movie. The trainee nurses have volunteered to take me this evening. When they arrive to collect me it is obvious that much preparation has gone into their make-up and choice of saris for the evening's entertainment. I feel a little self-conscious in my usual tatty garb. Arriving at the venue, I'm struck by the similarities with some movie shows in outback Australia. The 'hall' is an open-sided affair and a large white cloth has been erected for the screen. My arrival causes some disturbance among the more senior citizens, who will not be satisfied until the 'mem-sahib' is provided with a very large and ungainly chair. Once I'm positioned in this throne, the show may continue. What follows is four hours of incomprehensible Tamil interspersed with an unbelievable action plot. Judging by my surrounding movie-goers it is a five-star performance. I lost the plot somewhere in the second hour when my bum went to sleep on this incredibly uncomfortable chair. If this is the local high life, I've had it.

*

A friend of mine from Australia turns up one day and creates much hysteria among the locals. Denis is the boyfriend of Margaret, my partner for 'Vegemite Wednesdays' back in Calcutta. He has decided to see India for himself and find out what Margaret and I have been raving about. I nearly weep with joy when I first clap eyes on him. We enclose ourselves in my lovely green room and I can feel the invisible eyes of the entire compound riveted upon my shutters. I decide to forget my promise and break open the bottle of Bundaberg rum that I have been virtuously hoarding for the past several weeks. Half a bottle later, after I have unburdened myself of every grievance and petty complaint I can think of, we decide to go into Trichy to see if there is any night-life. First, though, I wander somewhat unsteadily across to the convent to let them know I'm escaping for the night. God only knows what they think I'll be up to!

Trichy, it must be said, is no hive of social activity. We manage to find a double room for a reasonable price and, following the directions in the Lonely Planet bible, make our way to the nearest bar. Tamil Nadu has very bizarre liquor laws designed to make the acquisition of alcohol as difficult as possible. A permit system is in place and fortunately I had the foresight to acquire one of these in Madras, when hope sprang eternal. Denis and I find a rather seedy, quiet bar and proceed to refresh both my memory and palate with the pleasures of ice-cold beer. Several bottles later I'm even looking fondly at Pulambaddy and my green room. We stagger out of there, hijack two cycle rickshaws (one of which I crash twenty metres later) and then beat a hasty retreat back to our room.

My chief task in the morning is to find a shop that sells tampons. My stock of this essential item is slowly diminishing. I did not think to bring a large supply with me as they are a readily available commodity in Calcutta. Denis and I venture into several chemist shops and when a thorough viewing of their stock reveals no tampons, the mere thought of trying to explain my request with a combination of Tamil and mime has me leaving the shops in fits of laughter, thus reinforcing the Indian perception that all foreigners are crazy. As a last resort I go to the general post office and pen a quick emergency letter home. Later I board the bus back to Pulambaddy, promising to catch up with Denis in October in Bangalore if my situation at Pulambaddy doesn't improve. One more month will probably be my limit.

*

I've been here about ten weeks now and while I'm beginning to feel a connection with the people, it is just too isolated for me to stay much longer. I am a people person and this lonely existence is starting to play on my mind. The work is interesting and I have certainly learnt a lot about leprosy but I've never been a great one for watching from the sidelines and desperately need a challenge both physically and mentally.

The greatest excitement in the last few weeks has been the delivery of a post-bag for me. The kitchen girls made a special trip to deliver this most unusual item. Once I recognised my mother's writing, its contents were immediately apparent. The bag had already suffered an inquisitive probing from somebody's finger, judging from the small hole at the end of it, and the girls chattered hopefully about lollies. As tactfully as possible I banished them from my room before opening the bag. My mother had performed wonders again and I'm safe in the sanitary department for several months to come.

I have also received a letter from Sister Luke enquiring when I will be joining them in Kalighat. I wrote to her shortly after arriving here and from the tone of her reply she is not in the least pleased that I have offered my services to a rival order. However, she seems to be in no doubt that I'll be returning to Calcutta soon. She's probably got the blue-bordered sari ready and waiting for my arrival. I long to be active and feel useful again, so decide that I will travel to Bangalore to see Sister Gentiana and find out if there is anything else I can do before I accept the inevitable and return to Calcutta.

Having made this decision I quickly pack up and prepare for departure. Saying goodbye to the nurses and leprosy workers is more emotional than I had imagined. Although my stay has been brief, we have all had quite a dramatic influence on each other. The biggest surprise of all is when the Sister Superior actually says that she will miss me. This has been the longest sentence she's spoken to me in ten weeks. I'm in no doubt that I'm the strangest female that any of them have ever come across.

 I decide to play tourist for a week and travel to Bangalore via a hill station west of Trichy named Ooty and Mysore, city of the pink palace and sandalwood. But after a few days of temples and tea gardens I discover that I'm not very good at this aimless wandering. People and their lives interest me more than buildings and history, so I hasten on to Bangalore.

This is a remarkable city by Indian standards and is the intellectual and technological driving force in modern India. It is a university city and thousands of students create a young, vibrant atmosphere. I eventually find a room in a run-down hotel, very crowded and overrun with all the usual nasties. I'm too exhausted to look any further, but will definitely shift tomorrow.

The next day I manage to track down Denis at a religious centre. He is supposed to be joining others from Toowoomba in some spiritual renewal workshop. His outlook has changed somewhat since his arrival in India and he now feels that he will gain more benefit from travelling further than from meditating. We extricate him from the course and rescue my backpack

from the fleapit hotel and book into a much cleaner,
more respectable establishment.

When we meet the others that afternoon, we find
they are laden with a cake and gifts for my twenty-
third birthday. I'm making a habit of having birthdays
in India. We celebrate on the roof of a local hotel and
it feels nearly like sitting in a beer garden back home.
My brother Richard has been at work with the tape
recorder again and while this particular production is
of a slightly better quality than the last, it still contains
the same characters, themes and music. Margaret is
on this tape lamenting the fact that she is not listening to it with me in the Y. Apparently it is much harder
to talk into the machine than to listen. I even learn,
via one of my cousins, that we have won the America's
Cup. Needless to say this world-shattering news never
made it to Pulambaddy. All this spoken English language and copious amounts of beer have me
dreaming about the peace of my little green room.

I go to meet with Sister Gentiana at the hospital in
which she is working, hoping that she may be able to
suggest something that will be more fulfilling for me
to do. Returning to Calcutta seems like a plan of last
resort as I really hoped to find something different
and rewarding to do this time in India. I have a great
fear that returning to Calcutta might shatter the
image of my 1981 experience. Memories are fragile,
particularly of such an explosive place.

Sister Gentiana is very busy with her own work and
study, but encourages me to hang around for a couple
of weeks while she attempts to find me a suitable
placement. Patience, however, has never been one of

my virtues and it is with much regret that I thank her for all her help and resolve to return to Calcutta after all.

Denis and I make our travel arrangements, he to visit Goa and me to return to Madras. During his travels so far Denis has certainly met some interesting people, one of whom gave him a large supply of marijuana. He is most generous with his gift and when we part I have a small supply in an empty Vegemite jar. Drugs of all description are freely available in this country and my last experience with the evil weed was in Calcutta. We were desperate to find a present for Robin, one of the volunteers. When I suggested some marijuana or hash the other girls thought this a good idea. We collected 100 rupees with which to make a purchase and repaired to Sudder Street where, within ten minutes, I'd purchased five small foil-wrapped balls of hashish. Back in the Y, I showed my prize to the other girls and we all marvelled at the bargain basement price of only one rupee per ball. Therese, Patty and I decided to test the merchandise before we gave it to Robin and spent the next couple of hours laughing uncontrollably in their room. If only our parents and the nuns could have seen us then. Needless to say, Robin enjoyed her birthday present very much and with the ninety-five rupees left over we were able to take her out to dinner as well.

Having finally made the firm decision to return to Calcutta, I decide to treat myself to a week on a beach before stepping back into the smog and filth. Mahabalipuram is a seaside town just south of Madras. It is here that I decide to recharge my batteries before tackling Calcutta again, but unfortunately I am struck down with fever upon arrival. I swallow half-a-dozen anti-malarial tablets, a few paracetamol and ride it out. A few days later the fever is gone and I can enjoy the beautiful beach and wonderful seafood that is here in abundance. The laid-back coastal atmosphere reminds me of Australia. The few other foreigners I encounter seem to spend most of their days smoking the dreaded weed. While I'm more than happy to join in occasionally, it is not my life's purpose to be stoned twenty-four hours a day.

I meet an interesting local Indian guy who introduces me to his guru and the art of third-eye meditation. This seems to entail sitting cross-legged and concentrating fervently on the spot between the two eyes. I find it really hard to concentrate, as a maniacal vision of Sister Luke keeps appearing before me. The spirituality and beliefs in India are a potent mixture and I'd really like to be able to study and gain some of the serenity that surrounds the truly committed believers. My energy seems to be mostly centred in the physical, and any mental energies get wrapped up with it.

All in all, this interlude has been invaluable in allowing me to make some sense of the Pulambaddy experience and prepare myself for a return to Calcutta. I am aware that returning to a place you once loved does not always live up to your expectations.

TWENTY-FOUR

 On boarding the train for Calcutta, I find myself assigned to the 'ladies only' compartment. This comprises a small room with three bunks on either side. The middle bunk folds up so that the occupants all have a seat during the day. I'm unsure if this compartment is a blessing or a curse as several ladies with vast amounts of luggage start to fill the space. The most beneficial aspect of being Western and wearing trousers is that I'm given the top bunk, as climbing up to these areas is a little difficult in a sari. The added benefit of the top bunk is that it is a fixture and so long as you don't wish to sit up, you always have somewhere to rest. Another feature of the ladies compartment becomes most apparent as we progress along the route and the other ladies pull the door shut and latch it against intruders. Space on any mobile conveyance in India is a hard-won prize and as the multitudes keep adding to the already laden train, our little oasis is staunchly guarded by the ladies below.

We travel for two days on the monotonously sway-ing coach, with numerous stops. The little I can see from my window is the never-changing vista of palm trees, rice paddies and villages, followed by a gradual build-up of houses and other buildings each time we approach a town. These dwellings, people's homes, are practically within reach as we thunder past. The other ladies and I exchange only a few words on this trip, but they have been most generous in sharing their enormous supply of food, drink and sweets with me. I gather from the way they talk and laugh that I'm quite a novelty item. I couldn't be more content, perched here in my lair, while they fight off the masses trying to find space, reducing the harassed conductor to a quivering mess. The power of women has never been more evident.

My main concern is Calcutta. Will it live up to my memories? The physical aspects of Calcutta will be as abhorrent today as they were two years ago, but will the magic still be there? Lying here on the train it seems like such a stupid question. I berate myself and start to list all of Calcutta's negative points. This takes an inordinate length of time and I consider abandoning ship at the next stop. I get all spiritual on myself and murmur, 'into your hands' etc. We must be getting close now; I can feel Sister Luke's emanations already.

*

I can sense Calcutta before I see it. It starts with a humid, smoky smell; eventually the taste of grit and a light dusty feeling on the skin is a dead giveaway. My first glimpse of the Howrah bridge almost has me in tears. It's just like coming home. Once I'm out of the station, on a bus and walking down Sudder Street I feel like I've never been away. I find a place in a five-bed room at the Modern Lodge, one of the many tourist hotels in the area. After a quick shower and change of clothes I prowl the streets soaking up the atmosphere and familiarity.

As the afternoon wears on, I find myself walking towards Chowringhee and its bus stops. I try to convince myself that I'd be better off resting and getting used to Calcutta but, like any addict, I have little control over myself as I board a bus for Kalighat. Walking down Kalighat Road my spirits soar as I glimpse the dun-coloured building on the corner. Entering Kalighat is almost like visiting a sacred shrine for me. As always, it's the pungent smell that hits you first, making you gag. How could I ever have romanticised this place?

I'm the only one here and I have time to quietly wander around the wards until Hazel, one of the Indian workers, recognises me and I'm whisked upstairs to see all the others. Maria, of heart operation fame, is looking healthier than ever and as I sit on her bed I'm deluged with twenty months of family happenings and general gossip. I greet and exchange stories with several members of the Kalighat roof families and while I'm chatting over tea and cigarettes the sisters arrive and the familiar sounds of frenetic activity announce the start of the afternoon shift.

Several cigarettes later I summon the courage to descend the stairs and face Sister Luke. I find her on the female ward, deep in discussion with several volunteers. Hazel grabs my arm and announces in top voice, 'Sister, Sister, Tracey has come back!' I've never been so embarrassed and can feel my face burning red. Sister Luke just grabs my arm and asks, 'What took you so long?' As she turns and presents me to the other volunteers their collective comment is, 'Oh! So you are the Tracey we've heard so much about.' God, I think to myself, what has Luke been saying about me and how much, if anything, has been the truth? I have probably been portrayed as 'a nun in the making', Sister Luke's favourite vision of my future.

Obviously the resident volunteer community is not entirely enamoured with the return of yours truly. Sister Luke doesn't help matters by immediately taking me under her wing. She escorts me on a tour of all the improvements made to Kalighat in my absence, the most startling of which is the repositioning of the cooking area to the middle section of the building and near the water tanks. She assures me that this new and improved construction does not explode and cover all the inhabitants in a shroud of smoke. Progress indeed.

The one permanent fixture of Kalighat is the patients and I swear to God that most of them look exactly the same as when I was here last. They are like generic models that come from some huge factory producing emaciated bodies with large brown eyes in sunken faces. It is only when you spend time with each individual that they can establish their own personality and humanity. It's a very sobering thought that nothing has really changed here and probably never will. Sister Luke, however, has an unquenchable passion and optimism for these people and her work, which inevitably breeds hope in my doubting mind.

The other volunteers seem surprised when I leave early and don't travel back with the sisters to the Mother House and adoration. I'm afraid that the religious aspects of the Missionaries of Charity are still not high on my list of priorities.

During the next few days I return to my normal Kalighat schedule of mornings and afternoons and slowly get to know some of the other volunteers. I try to avoid all the medical jobs and keep out of Sister Luke's way as I settle back into the language and pace of Kalighat. I find like-minded souls on the roof and, as we drag smoke down into our lungs, I hear about the picture Sister Luke has painted of me. This rose-tinted description would amaze my mother and leaves me speechless. True to form, Sister Luke has rein-vented me as a young missionary in the making, anxious to answer the call. I regale the volunteers with a few of my more outlandish exploits and social high-lights from 1981. They visibly relax, their united wariness evaporates and I gain some acceptance.

The settling-in period is going better than I expected, and as I move about Calcutta I sometimes feel as if I have never left. All I really need now is to find some sort of social life. Coffee and meals with the other volunteers in Sudder Street is a great way of get-ting to know people but in my heart I'm aching for a wild night out in one of the many clubs in Calcutta. It is with this in mind that I plan to hit the Marine House on Friday night and see if anybody I know is still here.

TWENTY-FIVE

 There is a particular look on the face of a nun who wants you to do something that you really want to avoid. Friday afternoon at 4.00 p.m. I encounter just such a look. The moment I arrive at Kalighat, Sister Berchmans pounces upon me, demanding to know why I'm late and informing me that they have an emergency. One glance at Sister Luke, and my long experience here and with other nuns, has my trouble antennae screaming. I know that whatever is about to come out of her mouth is definitely not something I want to hear. With my mind already settled on the word 'No' I nearly miss it when she informs me that I'm going to Patna at 5.00 p.m. This is such an amazing pronouncement that I'm left temporarily speechless, only delivering my response when Sister Luke has turned back to her preparations for the journey.

Sister Berchmans fills me in on the whole story, continuing to ignore my adamant refusal to go anywhere. One of our patients is a young man named Kumar who has been with us for several days. He is very close to death and has just been discovered here by his father and brother. They wish to take him home

143

to his mother and family. Patna is a thirteen-hour train journey into the neighbouring state of Bihar. The sisters have agreed to the trip and graciously offered two Western nurses to accompany Kumar. The other unfortunate volunteer is Iain, a British nurse, obviously a novice when dealing with nuns. While I feel for Kumar's parents, I have been looking after him for the past few days since my return and I'll be amazed if he lasts the journey to Howrah Station let alone Patna. I know that Sister Luke is also of this opinion by the way she continues to avoid me.

How to describe Kumar's condition? We don't really deal in diagnoses at Kalighat but rather a symptomatic treatment of the various conditions that each person presents with. Kumar was picked up by the council and arrived here in rags and semi-conscious. He is grossly emaciated, a condition emphasised by his very long body. His hair has been shaved off to manage his lice and this only accentuates his sunken facial features; the bones almost seem to pierce his skin. Large brown eyes flutter open occasionally. Diarrhoea, vomiting and malnutrition have caused dehydration and rapid physical deterioration. We have managed to control these symptoms to a small degree but his overall condition has not improved. He has some form of major intestinal infection which is not responding to any treatment. He is eighteen years of age and looks eighty.

The sisters use every devious weapon in their arsenal to cajole me, and somewhere between the emotional blackmail and the bribery, I concede defeat. As a quid pro quo I have their solemn oath to devote endless hours of prayer to the resumption of my full and satisfying social life once the present mission has been accomplished.

Sister Berchmans organises a box with a few essentials for our trip, which include cheese sandwiches, apples, bananas and the largest container of water I've ever seen. Sister Luke, Iain and I assemble a few medical supplies in another box. We throw in bags of intravenous fluid, needles and cannulas, naso-gastric tubes and medications, as well as a supply of clean linen. It has been decided that Kumar will be transported on his mattress from Kalighat. We load him and all our supplies into the ambulance and hang on for dear life as the driver tries to break all known speed limits in Calcutta in his attempt to deliver us to Howrah Station by five o'clock. If this doesn't kill poor Kumar, nothing will.

Arriving in one frazzled piece at Howrah, the driver decides that he must park his precious ambulance right on the platform. Once the right platform has been ascertained we drive in and plant ourselves firmly in the middle of it. The journey gets off to a predictably auspicious start when we are informed that the train won't leave until nine o'clock. God, I knew this was a bad idea. While this news has Iain and I fuming with exasperation, the Indians in our party just shrug their shoulders and say, 'What to do?' This is the universal response to all small and large problems in this country and is usually followed by a cup of tea. Iain and I leave Kumar to the sisters and, anxiously reaching for our cigarettes, we head for the closest tea stall.

I haven't had much of a chance to chat with Iain prior to this. All I know is that he has just completed his training and that this is his first trip here. I try to give him the benefit of my hard-learned, cynical wisdom and assure him of the lunacy of our impending disaster. This is his first experience with nuns. We both hope with all our hearts that we can deliver Kumar safely to his family but have to acknowledge that the likelihood of success is very remote. The reason we have been chosen for the journey, rather than a couple of sisters, is that we are trained nurses. We are also travelling in the company of men, Kumar's father and brother. This is out of the question for the sisters, though my virtue is obviously not a consideration. To top it all off, Sister Luke pointed out that we wouldn't be missed as we are independent volunteers. Subtlety has never been her strong suit.

It would be an understatement to say that our whole troupe causes something of a spectacle in the station; a small initial crowd has now grown to number hundreds as speculation about our presence travels round the station. All the disruption and moving about have caused Kumar's diarrhoea to start up again with a vengeance. This is the most offensive and foul-smelling discharge I have ever encountered. There are some smells that you can get used to in nursing, but this even has Sister Luke gagging as we change his pants and sheet. We have to move Kumar out of the ambulance and lay him on the platform in the hope of finding some fresh air. Needless to say, one obviously dying man, complete with drips and tubes, two nuns in blue-bordered saris, two foreigners and a couple of Indians make for great entertainment for the ever-growing crowd.

Kumar's father is having great trouble in persuading the train conductor and his several colleagues to allow Kumar on the train. One look at this poor boy was enough to make them refuse permission. We throw our heavy ammunition into the battle and Sister Berchmans strides over to sort him out. Having witnessed her negotiating skills previously, I ready Kumar for the trip. Thirty minutes later she returns and directs us to a carriage. I feel great empathy for the conductor as we manoeuvre past him; the poor man is looking a few shades paler and much less sure of himself now. We lay Kumar on a bunk directly outside the ladies compartment, which we four will occupy, and hopefully he will get a reasonable cross breeze here. The other passengers are far from happy with our presence and try to keep as much distance as possible.

When we are finally ready for departure Sister Luke takes me aside for some last-minute instructions. She gives me 200 rupees for our return tickets and expenses, which is just as well because all Iain and I possess are the clothes we are wearing, a few rupees and half-a-pack of cigarettes. Then she quietly drops her bombshell. 'If Kumar should die on the journey,' she says, 'you must pretend he's still alive, otherwise you may all be thrown off the train.' I knew my instincts had been right from the start. She then tells me that all the sisters will be praying for our safe arrival. This does not reassure me as I board the train and wonder for the thousandth time what the hell I am doing here in Calcutta.

We begin our journey with Iain, me, Kumar's father and brother perched on the edges of our seats in the ladies compartment, anxiously observing the rise and fall of Kumar's chest. As the trip progresses we slowly relax and, over endless cups of coffee and continuous cigarettes, Iain and I learn a little of Kumar's history. He has just finished school and comes from a well-to-do family in which his father and two of his brothers are lawyers. As the youngest of a large family Kumar has always been the favourite and somewhat indulged. He argued with his father about going to university and then ran away from home. The most horrifying part is that he only left eight weeks ago. Young people that run away from home have to face similar problems in any society and some are better equipped for living on the streets than others. I have come to know many street people in Calcutta during my time here and it certainly takes great courage, ingenuity and cunning to just scratch out an existence. The skills required for this harsh and unforgiving life are not something that a young middle class man from a small town would know. The speed with which Kumar has been transformed from a healthy young man into the near-corpse I see before me now is frightening, and makes the shock and horror his father and brother are going through all the more understandable.

The endless movement of the train seems to make Kumar more restless, and we each take turns at sitting with him. The feelings of disquiet in our carriage grow with each influx of passengers as we stop at every station along the way. We try to shield Kumar from them and I give one of my more imposing white 'mem-sahib' performances each time I leave the ladies compartment and attend to Kumar with an air of confidence that I certainly don't feel. The hours pass with agonising slowness and Iain and I are forced to change Kumar and his bedding when the rancid fumes alert us that diarrhoea has struck again. This procedure has understandably heightened the sense of fear and anger in the other passengers, but thankfully has also kept them well away from us. While the actual process of cleaning and changing Kumar presents us with no problem, Iain and I are left holding the most offensive and foul sheet and pants imaginable. After the very briefest of ethical discussions, I hasten to the door and jettison the offending articles on the rail tracks. My qualms about possibly spreading a contagious disease across Bihar are overpowered by the relief of drawing in a lungful of reasonably fresh air. I hope to God the sisters are working overtime on the prayer business tonight.

We finally arrive in Patna around ten o'clock the next morning. Kumar has somehow survived this far and, although still semi-conscious, his condition has not deteriorated dramatically. Our first major task is to get him off the train. Iain and I, carrying our precious cargo, are practically exploded out the door as the will and muscle of the people behind us overpower the dozens of people trying to clamber into the carriage. By some mysterious stroke of luck, Iain has control of the top half of the mattress while I have the bottom. We have to carry Kumar up the steps, across the bridge and down the other side to where Kumar's father has a taxi waiting. Iain and I carry the boy side on, our arms fully extended under him. As we slowly ascend the steps the inevitable happens and I soon have the honour of feeling Kumar's diarrhoea running down the front of my trousers. By this stage Iain and I are suffering from nervous exhaustion, not to mention caffeine and nicotine overload, and are determined that nothing will impede our mission. Needless to say Iain finds my revolting predicament most amusing. Once we have conquered our own little version of Mount Everest, Kumar's father is anxious that we get Kumar home as quickly as possible to see his mother.

Arriving at the modest two-storey house, we carefully unload Kumar and carry him upstairs to his waiting family. As we lower him to the floor his mother prostrates herself over him. Her wailing and obvious shock and grief cause tears to start pouring down my face. With the love and tenderness that only a mother can show, she and her daughters wash and clean Kumar and dress him in his own clean clothes. We wait at the house only thirty minutes and then take Kumar to the local hospital. Having brought him this far I am now fervently hoping that with some intensive medical treatment he may return to his family completely.

The Patna General Hospital is no world-beating establishment but it is equipped with a laboratory and qualified doctors. The admitting doctor is not thrilled with our presence and even less enthusiastic about our patient. He certainly does not hold out much hope but with quite a bit of pressure from Iain and me he does order blood tests. My confidence is further dampened when the person taking the blood cannot find a vein. Frustration gets the better of me and, grabbing the needle and syringe, I take the samples for him. Months of trying to find veins on the collapsed people in Kalighat have at least given me some skills. We finally and reluctantly leave Kumar in the care of the hospital staff, with his mother keeping vigil beside him. Iain and I return to the family home where we are treated as honoured guests and given most refreshing cold glasses of beer and a sumptuous meal. By now we both feel like a part of this large and warm family. We stay only a short time so that they can all return to the hospital and Kumar.

Iain and I then catch a taxi to the local Mother Teresa establishment and, after we have produced a letter from Sister Berchmans, a very sceptical nun allows us inside. The sister in charge gives us the once-over and it is at this point that I remember our dishevelled appearance and my reeking trousers. Once we have explained ourselves and our mission, she suggests with a smile that we might like a wash. Unfortunately they don't have any fresh clothes that would fit us, and while the stench of my pants is horrendous the mere thought of wearing a sari has me thinking of Sister Luke and how I'd like to kill her. A quick wash in a bowl of cold water and a good scrub with the soap has me somewhat restored to the land of the clean. The sister then suggests that Iain and I lie down for a rest before we leave for the station and our return journey to Calcutta. I am reduced to hysterical laughter as she directs me to the Patna version of the home for the dying. I receive a bed in the female section and Iain in the male. I always knew I'd come to a bad end but hadn't quite imagined this one. It is impossible to sleep but I lie on my bed and relive the past twenty-four hours and am once more amazed at the unpredictability of living and working in Calcutta.

Around five o'clock we return to the station and it is with great joy that we meet two of Kumar's brothers. They have returned to buy our tickets and make sure that we catch the right train. At this point I decide to take advantage of Sister Luke's money and offer to buy everyone a few drinks. We find a suitable hole-in-the-wall bottle shop and, clutching large bottles of beer, we all toast each other in endless declarations of love and friendship. Our euphoria continues all the way to the platform—until another brother finally finds us and tells us that Kumar has just died. I feel the bottom drop out of my world and just sit down on the platform and cry. All the brothers thank us for everything and then leave. Iain and I just look at each other and by unspoken agreement start to drink the half bottle of whisky that we had bought for the return journey. We finish it with incredible speed but the sense of failure still haunts both of us.

When we finally board the train it is impossible to find a seat and we crouch wherever we can find space. By this stage of the game I've given up on ever feeling clean again. Exhaustion and alcohol combine to numb my mind, but each time I start to fall asleep I am stepped on or jostled by one of my hundreds of fellow travellers.

Another tiring thirteen hours later Iain and I walk back into Kalighat to deliver our news to Sister Luke. She is delighted to hear that we arrived safely but is less concerned over the final outcome. She even has the hide to graciously grant us a day off. As I wander back down Kalighat Road. I wonder if I ever want to come back again.

TWENTY-SIX

 I have physically recovered from the Patna experience and have consigned my emotional scars to the ever-increasing pool of experiences that are best left to mend themselves. Back once again at Kalighat I resume my usual routine and concentrate my thoughts on trying to establish some form of social life. As Friday looms closer I happen to run into an Irish volunteer named Ita. It turns out that she arrived in Calcutta several months after I left in 1982, and had the great fortune to meet Norman and a few of the others that I knew during my time here. My fame has spread before me and she is more than willing to take me to the Marine House on Friday and introduce me around. The most compelling news that Ita gives me is that the Marines' Ball is on again in a couple of weeks.

I quickly chase down Sister Berchmans, remind her that she owes me several thousand prayer sessions, and instruct her to put all spiritual effort into the chance of a ball ticket coming my way. I leave Sister Luke out of it as she probably feels that any return to the extravagant social engagements that I enjoyed so much last time will only draw me further away from the convent. Unfortunately, Sister Berchmans' excitement is unbounded and she is loudly anticipating our next shopping adventure and planning possible dress designs. Obviously her faith in success is greater than mine.

Returning to the Marine House I enter warily, hoping against hope that I may meet the same sorts of warm, fun-loving people that I encountered here in 1981. Without those friends and the variety they brought to my life, I don't think I'd have survived. Ita introduces me to a group of men and I quickly discover that they are working at one of the car plants in Calcutta, designing a new car, the Contessa, for the Indian market. They are a mixture of Englishmen and Scotsmen and soon have me in fits of laughter as they describe their first six months on this project. These guys are very similar to the men I met last time and are suffering from the same frustrations and culture shock that all working Westerners feel. During the evening we all swap disaster stories and, over several bottles of beer, exchange family details and personal histories as only foreigners flung together in a foreign land will. Being Australian among a group of British is not always easy but I am able and willing to give as good as I get.

While I spend most of the evening with the car brigade I have an opportunity to meet a few of the marines and discover that the entire group that was here in 1981 has been transferred elsewhere. The physical layout and Friday night parties are the same as always; it's just a whole new set of players now.

As the evening progresses, I ask Ian (leader of the car team) and the lads about the ball. They inform me that they all have invitations but are unsure if they'll attend. I describe my last Marines' Ball and they quickly decide that it might be fun after all. I then ask bluntly if anyone would like a partner for the evening and also offer Ita as a suitable candidate. Chivalry is not dead—Ian and Robert offer themselves up for the slaughter. Sister Berchmans will be pleased, but I think I'll keep her in suspense for another week at least. The whole night is a wonderful release and as I wander home to my bed I feel more alive than ever.

Ten days later Sister Berchmans bubbles over with pride in her prayer abilities when I inform her that I'm going to the ball. She delivers a thump to my back as she pronounces, 'I told you so,' and starts to discuss shopping and dresses. I have to gently calm her down, pointing out that as it is only four days till the ball, I'll have to buy a ready-made outfit. She is disgusted with me and it is only now that I realise how much my forays into the outer world provide the nuns with a diversion from the everyday Kalighat experience. I promise to give a full description after the ball and hopefully provide a few photos as well.

I buy a very nice Punjabi ensemble for only 65 rupees and it looks every bit as glamorous as my last outfit. It has black pants and a long red, silver and black over-dress. The boys pick us up and it's off to the ballroom at the Grand Hotel once more. I revel in the opulence and partake of every drink and delicacy on offer. The Cinderella effect is even more pronounced this time as I remember my last three

Tracey and friends at her second Marines' Ball

months in the south of India. Calcutta and this lifestyle allow you to pretend to be anything you wish to be. I dance, eat, drink and talk the night away, and while I don't end up at the Marine House at 6.00 a.m. again, I nevertheless have a wonderful night and meet many other expatriates living here in Calcutta.

I give Sister Berchmans and all at Kalighat a glowing account of the ball and over the next few weeks the number of social occasions that I attend starts to climb. I'm once again a regular Thursday evening participant at the British High Commission bar and I've been back to Tollygunge with all of its splendours. Walking down Park Street one day I even run into a couple of Indian men that I knew before and they immediately ask me out for dinner. God, I love this city.

 It is two months since my return to Calcutta and my social life has climbed back to the glorious pinnacle that I achieved in 1981. I continue to work at Kalighat every morning and most afternoons, and in many respects it's like I've never been away. My nocturnal activities are a source of much discussion among some of the volunteers, who are continually amazed that I remain in Sister Luke's good books despite my obvious lack of religious zeal and preference for partying. I just tell them that I minister to the poorest of the poor during the day and the richest of the rich at night. I'm an equal opportunity volunteer!

However, this lifestyle is not what I had planned for my return to India and I'm constantly searching for other avenues in which to work. I've visited all of Mother Teresa's homes in Calcutta, and while many other volunteers work in these places the only home for me is Kalighat. It is the only place where I feel completely confident in my abilities and that I make a positive contribution. I still dream of working with lepers, and after my brief experience in Pulambaddy I would hope to have something to offer in this direction. Sister Luke is absolutely horrified by my desire. For a woman who has seen every possible affliction and example of human misery come through her door, she has an unnatural fear of lepers. She certainly believes it is right and proper that they should be cared for, but not by her and not by me. Every leper that finds their way to the Kalighat doors is immediately transferred to the leprosarium at Titigar. The brothers run this establishment and female volunteers are discouraged. I certainly won't be receiving any help from Luke in making this my suitable alternative to Kalighat.

I hear about a leprosarium outside Calcutta run by the Leprosy Mission people and go to visit. It is a huge undertaking and hundreds of lepers have moved here to avail themselves of its services. Whole villages have been established and the mission is staffed by doctors, nurses and physiotherapists. It is an impressive organisation and caters to both the medical and rehabilitation needs of the lepers here. Once again it is obvious to me that the Indians are best placed and equipped to deal with these people. I return to Calcutta uplifted by seeing such a progressive establishment but once again searching for a different role for myself in India.

*

The volunteer community is thrown into sudden turmoil when we are all asked to go to the Mother House for a special meeting. The West Bengal government has never been very happy about the number of foreign volunteers working for Mother Teresa in

Calcutta. We are all contributing to the portrayal of Calcutta as a backward, poor and undesirable destination. This is certainly not the perception that the West Bengal government wishes to convey. They are convinced that we are subversives, that we channel foreign funds into the country and avoid their regulations. The concept of reasonably poor Westerners working for nothing is beyond their comprehension. Most volunteers live in very basic accommodation, conserving their money as best they can, and as such don't contribute a lot to the economy of Calcutta. Commonwealth country volunteers do not require a visa to enter India, but all others do. They are granted three-month visas, which may be extended for a further three months. It is common knowledge among the volunteers that when renewal time comes round it is best to apply outside West Bengal as anyone applying in Calcutta is refused. Some volunteers have even been refused entry at the airport if they state on their immigration card that the reason for visiting is to work with Mother Teresa.

Sister Luke is beside herself with dread as she informs us that we cannot work at Kalighat until the problems with the police are worked out. There is a special branch of the police that deals with visas and immigration problems and they have apparently sent some message to Mother Teresa.

About thirty of us arrive at the Mother House and we are all directed to the chapel. Mother arrives, and after the obligatory prayers she begins to give us a talk. Anyone who has ever had any dealings with Mother or seen her on television will know that she talks softly and often in little parables about God's love and similarly spiritual matters. We are all finding it difficult to work out what our position is regarding working here in Calcutta and after several minutes of her talk someone asks if we all have to leave. As is the Indian way, Mother gives us neither a positive nor negative response, and we all look at each other even more perplexed. Mother tells us eventually that the police would like volunteers not to stay too long, but doesn't actually tell us how long is too long. Trying to steer us in other directions she tells us that we all have problems in our own countries and suggests that maybe we might be needed at home if any of us have someone 'mental' in the family! This particular notion has me and several others rolling around the floor in laughter as we try to find the lunatic among us. Again one of the volunteers tries to pin Mother down as to whether we have to leave, but she says no, just move around a little.

Next day at Kalighat Sister Luke wants to know what Mother has told us. We are still somewhat confused about the outcome of the meeting, but after considerable probing Sister Luke concludes that as Mother didn't expressly tell us to leave we are free to continue on at Kalighat. I'm not sure that this is exactly what Mother intended, but by now we have all identified our mental family member and realised it is us, so a little more convoluted logic makes perfect sense.

*

I have amazed the other volunteers with my selfless dedication to the patients of Kalighat by humbly offering to remain here and care for them while the newer volunteers all attend the annual children's picnic. Their enthusiasm and excitement over the picnic provokes a few guilt pangs and almost persuades me to share my insider knowledge. Then I reason that everyone should have at least one children's picnic to remember. But never two.

The morning is an exact repeat of my last picnic, and it is with a huge sigh of relief that I wave those naive, smiling white faces off on their buses.

Kalighat without Sister Luke, volunteers and dozens of sisters is finally a place of peace. I've got to know most of the patients reasonably well, and after giving out the medications, administering injections and completing the dressings I finally have time to sit and talk with some of the men. Cigarettes are not normally allowed in Kalighat but I'm soon on my way to buy dozens of the small Indian cigarettes called *bedis*. I distribute these to anyone with enough lung- and will-power to smoke them and within minutes we're all happily puffing away. Only another smoker knows the benefit of a relaxing drag. The women are now feeling excluded so I make another trip to the shop and soon have the entire building suffused with smoke. During my time at Kalighat I've been asked by different patients to supply anything from *bedis*, hashish, alcohol and opium. Unfortunately the most my limited resources can stretch to is the occasional *bedi*.

I return to the YWCA for lunch and a rest and make my way back to Kalighat at 3.00 p.m. When I hear the rumble of buses I take up a strategic position on the roof to witness the return of my fellow volunteers. From my vantage point the disappearance of the kids once they leave the buses is even more dramatic, as though they just evaporate into the crowd. I can't help smiling as I observe the very pale and drawn faces of the volunteers as they carefully descend from the buses. Dishevelled and disordered, they look as if they've just emerged from a war zone. Sister Luke and the other sisters are smiling, so I gather that yet another children's picnic has been deemed a great success. The volunteers are not impressed with my smiling face and some of them seem to think that the least I could have done was warn them, but I hold firm to my belief that everyone deserves at least one children's picnic. Once again my saint status has been severely damaged.

 I have finally decided to leave Calcutta, where I feel I am just marking time. An American girl named Carol has heard about a French-Canadian organisation that is looking for volunteers, and their fields of work are dispensaries, children and leprosy. It sounds like an answer to my prayers. Carol and I meet with Jean, the main man, and he gives us a broad outline of the group and its work. He explains that, as a new organisation, they only have a few centres. Their main base of operations is in a place called Kasauli which is in Himachal Pradesh, in the foothills of the Himalayas. I'm swept up in the excitement of it all and within the week Carol and I are rocking along on the train.

My ears are still ringing from the daily lectures that I have received from Sister Luke after I had the temerity to drop my bombshell. The fact that I was leaving for another organisation was treason enough, but to actually align myself with a non-Catholic outfit was beyond comprehension. She will be praying for my soul and a speedy return to the bosom of Kalighat.

I don't know Carol very well and as the hours slowly pass, I discover that her main interests are spiritual.

She is a registered nurse but her primary reason for coming to India is to experience the different religions and styles of meditation. I nearly jump off the train when she pulls out her crystal on a chain and starts asking it questions. This thing is apparently called a *dousa* and, depending on which way it swings, you can receive a negative or positive response to your question. Apparently the swing of the *dousa* made her decide to go to Kasauli. To think that I have nothing to blame my madness on!

Thirty-six hours later we find ourselves on a bus winding its way precariously around the mountains. The scenery is more beautiful than I could ever have imagined. Coming from a mainly flat country, the absolute majesty and size of these mountains is mind-blowing. On this glorious, fine day we can see the Himalayas in all their snow-clad beauty. I feel I could almost reach out and touch them. It is only when our driver careens around one of the perilous hair-pin turns and I am suddenly slammed against the window that I am forced to focus on the terrifying drop below us. All the other passengers are dozing placidly in their seats as Carol once again consults her *dousa* to verify our safety.

Kasauli is a small town, and as it is January and winter the houses and streets are covered in a light fall of snow. It is a perfect picture-postcard winter setting. Jean and Phillippe are there to meet us and take us to a house where they have the two top rooms, with a bathroom and shower below and a separate small building as a kitchen. There is one other volunteer called Helene, a French Canadian nurse. She works

The snow-covered lodgings in Kasauli: at least a beautiful area in which to
have a bad experience

here at the dispensary, while the boys are based in
Mussoorie. Claude, the man in charge, is away at the
moment and we decide to take a few days to settle
down before we work out where we'll best fit in.

My most pressing concern is the cold. I am wearing my only pair of jeans, several T-shirts and a cotton
jacket and I'm freezing to death. I'm the only one
among us with absolutely no experience of snow and
cold conditions. Helene takes me down to the storeroom where she produces dozens of boxes all full of
clothes donated by the good people of France and
Canada. I select long-johns, socks, jumpers, beanie,
scarf and gloves, and complete this outfit with an

Indian shawl that resembles half a blanket. I am now ready for the outside world.

We girls share a room with one small electric bar heater for warmth while the guys have the other room. Over the next couple of days we spend much of our time cramped into the small kitchen which boasts a few marvels of modern technology, namely a kerosene pump burner and an antique side-action toaster. Thank God for French men and their ability to cook. They try to impart their knowledge to me but I'm hopeless in a kitchen—though more than happy to eat the products of their labour. Claude has not returned but Jean and Phillippe must go back to Mussoorie. Carol gives the crystal a swing and decides to accompany them. My stomach leans heavily in this direction also, but I feel I must stay here with Helene. She has only been in India a month or so and is most unsure about the whole experience.

Claude eventually returns and the more I learn about this set-up the weirder it sounds. We open the dispensary from 11.00 a.m. till 1.00 p.m. and that is the extent of work accomplished. This is a rural area and while you would never say it is prosperous, it is certainly not poor. We only see about ten to twelve people a day, mostly mothers with children looking for free clothes. Claude directs me to a leprosarium nearby, giving me the impression that they will be providing funds and assistance to places like this. My visit reveals that this is a very well-run government institution and that they have never heard of Claude or his organisation. It is a lovely group of double-storey buildings set amongst the trees and in a previous existence was a tuberculosis sanatorium for the English. I ask a few of the lepers if there is anything they require and they tell me they would appreciate a soccer ball or volleyball. Not the most extravagant request I've ever heard of and I pay for this one myself. Clearly these patients lack for nothing; I'd be pretty content here as well.

Helene and I spend each morning at the dispensary and gradually she tells me more about Claude and the organisation. It has been founded by Monique, a French-Canadian and spiritual mother whose philosophy seems to be based on Hindu meditation and social work. When Helene tells me that we are supposed to pray each day to some prophet named Satiannanda, and meditate to tapes prepared by Monique, I'm out the door in minutes searching for the closest Catholic church. Thank God the Catholics made it to Kasauli and have a small but thriving congregation. I suddenly become a daily mass attender and tell Claude that my beliefs are very strong. If only Luke could see me now, she'd have that blue-bordered sari out in a minute. My disillusionment with this crowd is growing daily.

*

I have been here for three weeks when Claude announces that he and I are going to visit a leprosarium. This trip takes us to a place called Ambala and here I once again discover a very well-run government operation. From a few remarks that Claude lets drop, I finally work out that the organisation has received money from some international leprosy fund for work they are supposedly doing here. He is expecting some inspectors to review their programs. Claude is now on a bizarre leper hunt so that he can find some likely-looking candidates to show the inspectors. I'm supposed to look convincing as the front person. We visit a few other likely spots and it's a blessed relief when Claude finally decides to return to Kasauli. Claude and the whole organisation are as crooked as they come. God only knows how much money people have donated to this bogus operation. This little adventure has convinced me that a return trip to Calcutta is my new top priority.

Helene is the only impediment. She joined up with this lot in Quebec, receiving only a one-way ticket and no money. She has been trying for several weeks to get her family to send funds for a return ticket and all attempts to contact Monique have drawn blanks. I use my new-found knowledge of Claude and his organisation to pressure him into providing Helene with at least a ticket home. As subtlety has never really been my forte, Claude quickly gets the message and disappears to Delhi to contact Quebec.

We receive a letter from Carol: she only lasted two days in Mussoorie before she got bad vibes and the crystal suggested moving on. Apparently the work with the children bears a striking resemblance to that with the lepers.

At least this is a beautiful area in which to have a bad experience, and while we wait for Claude's return, Helene and I play tourist and wander around the foothills. The clean, fresh air is certainly a welcome relief from the smog and congestion of Calcutta.

Simla is only a few hours away and as I've read so many books about this summer capital of the Raj, I just have to see it. As our snow-covered bus crawls into the town I realise why I never read about Simla in the winter, it's absolutely freezing and everything is white. The novelty of snow and its beauty has worn off by now. We make for the closest hotel and drink coffee until the bus makes the return journey. It's one of those been-there-done-that type of episodes.

In fact this whole winter experience is wearing very thin. I've only managed to have a wash once a week and that has certainly not been a treat. I warm a bucket of water over the kerosene burner and when it is finally hot I make a mad dash to the bathroom. As an experienced bucket bather, I pour a couple of cupfuls of water over my head and then soap, shampoo and rinse. This procedure works fine in Calcutta but here in the mountains the water is cold by the time it reaches your navel. I hop around on frozen feet, yelling every curse I've ever learnt, then dress in the winter gear again and wash my clothes with the now almost cold water. I bring less zeal to this enterprise than normal, and return to the room to hang up my clothes, pondering the perils of frostbite as I try to restore some life to my frozen hands in front of the bar heater. Calcutta looks more like a paradise each day.

Claude finally returns with assurances that a plane ticket will be provided to Helene. She has also heard from her family and they will send her money if required. I don't like to leave her here but she assures me that everything will be all right. I board the bus and then train for Calcutta thankfully and, once ensconced on my third-tier berth in the second class carriage, I feel free at last. It is a great relief to have escaped the dishonesty of Claude and his lot. It doesn't even worry me when the exuberant Chandigar Judo team, spotting my white face among the multitude, begin eagerly trying to practise their English. I get so caught up in their youthful enthusiasm that I soon find myself doing a rather loud but toneless rendition of 'Waltzing Matilda' while standing in the aisle of the carriage. It's the first and last time in my life that I've ever received a resounding burst of applause. I even act as tourist information service for the Chandigar team and fill them in on all the attractions in Calcutta for this, their first visit.

I return to Kalighat feeling more stupid and gullible than anything else. Sister Luke only says, 'I knew you would be back. Your place is here.' The other volunteers have a great laugh about my adventures and over the coming weeks make up all sorts of jokes about incense, leper hunts and snow. It's nice to be back among the family again.

TWENTY-NINE

Settling back into Calcutta is difficult as my immediate problems are lack of money and suitable accommodation. I send a plea home to my mother for money and in the meantime I move from a dormitory bed in the Modern Lodge to a single room at the Paragon Hotel. It costs only 15 rupees a night but is no bigger than most cupboards. It has two half-doors which only open seventy degrees before hitting the bed. Through a simple act of contortion you can gain access to the interior, which contains a bed, and a fan standing on a very small table. No room for an overhead fan in this little box. Entry and exit is facilitated by standing on the bed.

Eating cheaply in Calcutta is not difficult but can take its toll on the digestive tract. Even Sister Luke takes pity on me when I start to look longingly at the food I'm feeding to the patients. She is a wonderful cook herself and contributes to my welfare with lunch most days at Kalighat. I maintain all my social contacts and never let the chance of a free meal pass me by.

Eventually my money arrives and I'm once again relatively secure in Calcutta. I move to the Salvation

Army hostel, sharing Room No. 16 with an Irish volunteer, Noeline. This is the pick of the rooms here, a three-bed room right on the roof of the hostel. It is only 10 rupees a night and we have a toilet and shower next-door which we only share with No. 17, a two-bed room. This is luxury and space at the bottom end of the market.

Noeline has been here for several months and works mornings at Prem Dan. She also works afternoons at Kalighat, has a wicked sense of humour and doesn't mind the odd gallon of alcohol either. We shall get along famously. Our third bed is eventually filled by a French volunteer, Michele, who completes our little home.

Through Noeline, I meet a group of Irish nurses who are working at various centres in the villages outside Calcutta. They work for an organisation called GOAL, mainly in maternal and child health. Two girls work in three different villages in cooperation with local projects. These include child immunisation programs and ante-natal care as well as running general clinics. They are organised through the Child in Need Institute here in Calcutta. It is refreshing to see real organisations in action.

The girls are only a short train trip away from Calcutta and they all try to gather in here every few weeks for a little R&R and to exchange progress reports. Our little haven at No. 16 can become very crowded when the Irish arrive. Noeline and I catch a train to the village some evenings whenever there is an excuse to have a party. My never-ending complaint about these visits is the complete lack of culinary expertise among the Irish. I've eaten potatoes and onions in every variation from fried to boiled and still they keep preparing them. Thankfully they are all excellent nurses and the immunisation of children and the ante-natal care of women is not dependent on their cooking skills.

One of the many effects of living in a foreign country is that we tend to romanticise our pasts. Unfortunately I come from a long line of truth stretchers and one night I find my mouth running away with itself describing my virtues as a cook in glowing terms. With no access to cooking facilities I feel reasonably secure in my deception. Some weeks later, however, the girls decide to call my bluff, and announce that the priest in charge of St Mary's church has offered us the use of his kitchen. As I find it extremely difficult to ever admit defeat, I plead for a few weeks' preparation while my devious mind plots some way out of my dilemma.

As always, I turn to Kalighat for an answer to my problem. I give both Sister Luke and Sister Berchmans a briefly edited version of my predicament and throw myself on their mercy. I even attend adoration in a desperate plea for help. The capabilities of the Missionaries of Charity are fully revealed the next day as we sit down to plan the menu. My complete ignorance on the topic is quickly revealed and I'm relegated to the sidelines. Grandiose plans are soon revised when we realise that I will have to actually cook some things and could spoil the entire meal. Simplicity seems safest, so we decide on soup, roast beef and vegetables. They have discovered several packets of English instant soup mix that even I can't bugger up. The sisters will choose and cook the beef and, with a little practice, even I should be able to manage the vegetables.

I fix the date for the dinner and as fate (or God?) would have it our third bed is now occupied by Reesa, a Jewish American girl who is actually an excellent cook. I take her into my confidence and swear her to secrecy. When D-Day finally arrives my plans are already in motion. I've given Sister Berchmans money to go to the markets at 5.00 a.m. and choose a prime piece of beef. Once at Kalighat I inspect the enormous lump of meat she has bought, and Sister Luke sets about her culinary duties. The meat is cooked in several smaller portions. When it is ready I wrap it in foil and place it in my bag. Sister Luke has even written out instructions for me. I travel back to the Sally Army on the bus, the aromas emanating from my bag almost causing a riot.

Back in No. 16, Reesa and I cannot control ourselves, so we devour one of my beef parcels. She reads the instructions and says, not a problem. At this stage I'm so pleased with myself that I decide to add a few items to the menu. Later that afternoon we go shopping and then set ourselves up in the kitchen. My additions consist of adding tomatoes and onions to the packet ox-tail soup, as well as garlic bread and a tin of mushrooms with cream and red wine sauce to go with the beef. I'm learning all sorts of amazing things during this dinner experience, one of which is that garlic has to be peeled. The more I open my mouth and utter yet another stupidity, the more Reesa rolls around the floor in fits of laughter. We can only manage to get three gas jets working and the operation of the oven is completely beyond us. We decide to sample some of the local Indian wine. Golconda red comes in a screw-top bottle and has a sharp and wrenching effect on the throat as it goes down, but after several large swallows you really don't notice. The soup is simmering away obediently, so we wrap the garlic bread rolls in foil, whack them in a big saucepan with a lid on, and hope they heat through. Reesa has the vegetables under control and we warm up the meat by the same method as the bread.

The girls have arrived and before they get too anxious I deliver the soup and place garlic rolls on each plate. The first course is an instant success and they keep saying that they never doubted me for a moment. Back in the kitchen Reesa and I are onto our second bottle of Golconda red. I splash a generous amount onto the mushrooms, add the cream and marvel at my own creation. The sauce does have that rather distinctive Golconda flavour, but by this stage Reesa and I have lost all sense of taste. Out go the main courses and we slowly sink to the floor, weak with relief and alcoholic paralysis.

One thing I knew for sure when I started this dinner was that it would be an outstanding success. There is nothing that is more guaranteed to please the Irish girls than a large helping of roast beef. The last time most of us tasted such a delicacy was in our own homes. Vegetarian India, the Missionaries of Charity, the home for the dying and destitute and Reesa have all combined to give me my one and only culinary triumph!

 When I arrive for work this morning I pass by the usual line-up of beggars that congregate outside the Kali Temple and for a reason I can't explain something makes me pause to investigate a small boy lying beside his mother. He is extremely hot to touch and, as I examine him further, I find that his respiration and pulse rate are galloping. Without hesitation or explanation I scoop him up and carry him into Kalighat. Sister Luke is on retreat for a fortnight and Sister Berchmans and I have the dubious honour of keeping Kalighat afloat. I place my small cargo on the floor and set about the task of finding him a bed. Fortunately someone died last night so there is a vacancy and I will not have to perform the Kalighat shuffle. I do upgrade the man from bed No. 32 (under the statue of Mary) to a bed further down the ward. Bed 32 is always reserved for the sickest patient and even the short move has given this man some hope of survival.

When Sister Berchmans speaks to the boy we discover that he is nine years old and named Raju. He is barely 90 centimetres tall and weighs next to nothing. The only large thing about him are his expressive brown eyes which seem to flicker between fright and exhaustion. Further examination indicates that he has pneumonia as well as the usual cocktail of malnutrition, dehydration, anaemia and skin infestations. We fear that his chances of surviving in hospital without his mother to help care for him are nil. Sister Berchmans has gone to speak with the mother and discovers that she is mentally disturbed and incapable of rational thought. I've had very little experience with treating children and pray that I don't make matters worse. I start with intravenous fluids, antibiotics and paracetamol, guessing the dosages required by a very, very small nine-year-old. We don't have anything as exotic as oxygen or a nebuliser but we're the only help this little fellow will get.

Within a few days Raju becomes the Kalighat mascot. Sisters, volunteers and patients have all taken to our youngest resident and he is being spoilt rotten. With just a few days of treatment he is like a new person. It is something that we rarely see around here and it has given us all a lift in spirits. Sister Berchmans has ransacked the donation boxes at the Mother House and Raju now wears T-shirts with Big Bird and other TV characters on the front. Volunteers and sisters alike bring him whatever he wishes to eat and slowly but surely his eyes regain a sparkle. Once removed from his drip he roams all over the place with amazing energy.

Eight days later, as I'm walking to Kalighat, I see Raju once again with his mother. Through limited communication, I understand that he feels responsible for her and that she needs him. Although my view of her maternal skills is low, there is nothing I can do. Kalighat certainly seems a little less sunny without him but this is really no place for a child. He returns to us a week later with diarrhoea and vomiting but once again leaves as soon as he recovers.

After that I continue to look out for him on the street. When he has been missing for a couple of days I ask his mother but she has no idea of his whereabouts. Another volunteer eventually recognises him at the orphanage run by the Missionaries of Charity and when I visit him there he's as happy as a pig in mud.

*

Sister Luke is back and this morning drags me off to a local hospital to visit a patient. Campbell Hospital is down near Sealdah railway station and we are to see a sister of one of the nuns who has fallen from a moving train. When we first see her I'm almost sick at the sight. She has massive head injuries and is lying on a filthy bed, still wearing the clothes in which she was admitted. Her head is swollen to twice its normal size, one eye is missing and her face is covered in stitches and dried blood. The only saving grace as far as I can see is that the poor girl is unconscious. She is one of many crammed into a dark and forbidding room without a nurse or relative in sight. Her relatives are very poor and live in a remote village miles outside Calcutta. It will be at least two days before they can get here.

We have brought all the necessary clothes, towels, soap and basin and while Sister Luke prepares the water I forage for a clean sheet. My skills in this department are excellent as I do not consider theft and/or lying to be inappropriate to these occasions. We clean away the blood and dirt and restore some semblance of humanity to this poor girl, but without proper medical attention she will surely die. She has a tracheostomy in place but it is so blocked with blood and other secretions she can barely breathe. I track down and commandeer a suction machine, so at least we can provide a clearer airway for her. An hour later we are on our way back to Kalighat. Sister Luke delivers her prognosis, 'No hope', and I'm left wondering yet again about the harsh realities of life and death in Calcutta. Two days later I see that face again, lying in her coffin during the funeral service at the Mother House.

*

There is so much physical suffering in Calcutta that those with mental illness receive very little help at all. In Kalighat each patient has a small file which records their name, age, religion, diagnosis and treatment. These pages are kept in a ring folder and written in pencil. Economy and recycling are mantras in Calcutta and each page can last through dozens of people. Those with any form of mental illness receive the all-encompassing description of 'mental' as their diagnosis.

It is to one such as this that I'm attending this morning and am tempted to add 'mad as a hatter' as well. The spaces on the record for name, age, etc. are all blank as the only response she gives to any question is to laugh hysterically. She is probably in her late teens, is malnourished and emaciated and has a moderate-sized swelling in her abdomen. Her body also carries the hundreds of scars that are testament to the brutality of life for those that are 'mental' in this society. I struggle to find her a physical diagnosis and lean heavily towards pregnancy or tumour as the most probable condition. Her treatment will remain a clean bed, clothes and three meals a day until further information comes to light.

Illumination is granted the next morning when I approach a more subdued young girl and an offensive odour tells me that all is not well. Hidden under the cover of blankets are two small foetuses, both perfectly formed and about 25 centimetres long. They were obviously stillborn, and once I check that the placenta is intact and any bleeding is minimal I remove them to the morgue. After a wash and a couple of breakfasts the young girl is once more back in Mad Hatter mode. Before the morning shift is over she has disappeared and God only knows when we'll see her again.

Another young girl in trouble, a relative of the Kalighat sewing lady, is admitted several days later. The sisters give her the royal treatment until it is discovered that her condition is the result of an abortion. Strict judgmental philosophies make this girl's existence here impossible so Noeline and I bundle her up to try our luck at the Assembly of God Hospital. We are seen almost immediately and over several cups of tea a lovely young Indian doctor tells us more about the methods of abortion used in India than I ever wanted to know. He admits Pria, and even stipulates 'no charge' on her admission form.

It is wonderful to see efficient medicine in practice. Blood tests and all manner of investigations are carried out on Pria and her treatment begins immediately. She is also lucky that she has family members who will help care for her in hospital. Noeline and I visit her every evening and within a week she is restored to normal health. I only wish that this standard of care could be given to all.

Yet another patient is screaming out for help and I find myself incapable of easing his pain. He is only a young man and has an enormous swelling of the scrotum. It is obviously an infection of some kind but the massive doses of antibiotics that I've given him have made no impression at all. He receives pethidine for the pain but this brings little relief. He implores me this morning to 'Cut, cut'. I fear the agony will drive the poor man mad before he dies. Despite the total lack of privacy in Kalighat, I decide to carry out some simple surgery. When I make an incision in his scrotum, I am almost rendered unconscious by the vile smell of the pus that discharges from his wound. I try to drain as much of this mess as possible and when I have finished I'm rewarded with the first smile I've ever seen on this man's face.

His name is Kamal and I carry thoughts of him and his condition with me for the next two days as no amount of scrubbing, soap or disinfectant will remove the smell from my hands. The drainage was only a temporary relief and within days we are back at square one. As a last resort I decide to take him to hospital.

Three hospitals turn us away and when I decide that the next one will be the last we finally meet a doctor who seems able to make a diagnosis. He tells me that it is Fornier's gangrene of the scrotum and is extremely difficult to treat. The hospital itself is the pits, but at least the doctor inspires confidence. Kamal doesn't want to stay but I buy a water container and glass, install him in a bed and promise to return the next day.

I return with high hopes only to find an empty bed. When I eventually find a nurse she informs me that Kamal committed suicide during the night by slashing his wrists with a broken glass. Guilt, blame and despair descend in mammoth quantities. He could have died at Kalighat with at least the semblance of people who cared about him.

Ego can be extremely dangerous when dealing with people's lives. I am responsible for this and can only hope that I have learned these are people before they are a disease.

THIRTY-ONE

The volunteer community is in a state of confusion once more. The police have been very active again and this time they have some justification. A recently arrived American volunteer has got herself mixed up with some drug peddlers. She has barely been here long enough to visit all of Mother Teresa's homes, let alone do much work, but the moment she found herself in trouble she claimed volunteer status and Mother Teresa's protection. Needless to say, Mother is not impressed and the rest of us are trying to keep a very low profile. This girl eventually leaves but the police continue to treat us all with suspicion.

In June the government announces that all people from Commonwealth countries will now require visas. When Sister Luke calls Noeline and I into the morgue one morning we know that bad news will follow. Because the morgue is the only quiet place in Kalighat it is here that Luke addresses us whenever she has something important to say. The poor woman looks completely destroyed as she tells us that we can no longer work here and that we must go to the police station at once. Sister Luke has come to know Noeline and me very well in the past several months and after she has delivered the bad news she makes both of us promise that we won't go out and hit the bottle. It is this parting piece of advice that sees Noeline and I collapse into fits of laughter as we both promise not to *hit* the bottle.

God, this is the second time I've been sacked from a voluntary job! Noeline and I return to No. 16 and decide to clear our room of all its empty bottles. When we have enough to fill my backpack and her bag, we set off to our local second-hand dealer and receive enough rupees for a few full bottles. Once our feeble attempts at room cleaning are completed we open a bottle of beer each and, so long as we refrain from any violent attacks on the bottles, we feel that our promise to Luke is intact. During the evening several other volunteers call to see us after receiving their marching orders. It also becomes apparent that Sister Luke has instructed some of them to check up on us to make sure we are keeping our promise.

There are very few volunteers in Calcutta at this time as it is the middle of the monsoon season and anyone with half a brain is elsewhere. Those of us who have to register at the police station meet in No. 16 to discuss our options. Patience is something that we have all learnt here and, as there are only seven of us, we decide to wait a few days in order to plan alternative strategies if we are told to leave immediately.

Our patience is rewarded when the police make a huge blunder by entering the Mother House during adoration, demanding to see a list of all volunteers. Their big mistake is in thinking that Mother Teresa has left Calcutta; they have committed the unforgivable by loudly interrupting adoration. Mother Teresa does not take this intrusion well at all and fronts the chief of police the next day, demanding an explanation. The up-side of all this is that we seven are to meet with the chief and work out any problems.

We arrive with Sister Maureen, the sister responsible for volunteers, and once we're all seated in the main office the chief of police, who looks most spectacular in his uniform, asks us all about our work and then says that we may have six-month residents' permits. We wander out of the building like survivors of a disaster, unable to believe that this emotional rollercoaster is over. As we all laugh with joy and relief we head to the closest bar to celebrate and redraw our future plans. None of us had considered the possibility that the government would allow us to stay.

*

Noeline has gone to Darjeeling for a brief holiday and when Adrienne, one of the Irish village workers, turns up looking for help, I'm it. She has come down with some sort of intestinal bug and she needs a replacement to go out to a remote village and help Edith with the immunisation program. Arriving in this village is like stepping back in time. The air is clear, the vehicles are few and everything runs at a slower pace. I have no idea what I'm supposed to do, but hope my ability to wield a needle and syringe will suffice.

My first surprise is that they still use glass syringes and steel needles. Edith tells me that they anticipate hundreds will attend the immunisation clinic and that glass and stainless steel are easiest to sterilise. Her living conditions are pretty basic, with one large room containing two beds, table and chairs and the ever-present kerosene pump cooker. A washroom, toilet and water pump are situated about twenty metres away.

We set off in the morning with all our supplies packed into a four-wheel drive vehicle. My second surprise occurs when we stop in the middle of nowhere and two three-wheeled bicycle carts appear. This is as far as the truck can go and the bicycles will apparently deliver us to the appropriate village. I eventually discover that it is safer and less bone-jarring if I walk beside my conveyance as roads are non-existent. When we reach our destination we are greeted by a sea of colour and an air of festival. The local health workers organise these days wonderfully and it creates an opportunity for the surrounding community to gather.

Edith and I set up our equipment in a small mud-brick room and before we begin the local organiser presents us with glasses of tea and a pack of cigarettes—obviously Edith's habits are well known in the area. We then begin the most amazing morning's work I've ever encountered. It is like working on a production line. The local health workers take care of all the paperwork and identification while Edith and I give the injections. The rationale behind this approach seems to be that it is better if the children equate pain with the transient foreigner than the local health worker. It becomes so hectic that I barely see a face, only skinny arms and bony buttocks. We have processed about 200 children when thankfully a halt is called for lunch.

Lunch is also something of a production. We are escorted to one of the more substantial-looking buildings in the area and, once inside and seated on the floor, an enormous number of dishes are placed before us. Hospitality is very important in India and we must force ourselves to eat as much as possible to save giving offence. My mouth explodes into a ball of fire as I inadvertently bite through a small but lethal chilli. My obvious distress and feeble attempts to quench the burning in my mouth afford our hosts great enjoyment. Once everyone in the vicinity has observed my performance someone gives me a bowl of curd which finally offers some relief. I am undoubtedly living up to all the villagers' conceptions about silly foreigners. Once lunch is finished we return to the business of immunisation and by the end of the day we have inoculated over 500 children. The sheer volume is mind-blowing. We pack all our equipment up again and make the return journey by cart and car. Our final duty before thankfully collapsing into bed is to sharpen the needles with a stone and sterilise everything in a pressure cooker ready for more children the next day. I dream about matchstick arms and emaciated buttocks all night long.

Four days later I return to Calcutta having jabbed my way through hundreds of children. I can't wait to get back to my own environment at Kalighat. Nevertheless I have enjoyed this new experience and I admire the Irish girls greatly. The entire immunisation program runs like a dream. It has been great to witness what can be done with genuine cooperation between the locals and a charity organisation.

THIRTY-TWO

 My Scottish friend, Ian, is going home. After two years of hard work they finally have a new Indian car in production. He has invited me out to his rooms at Tollygunge to scavenge among the things he's leaving behind. I have become an expert in the art of making use of other people's rubbish. Ian's collection includes foreign soap, shampoo, deodorant, toilet paper, razors and an assortment of medicines. I bag the lot and even linger over the smell of lime soap, mentally casting aside my block of Lifebuoy. I leave the clothes and stationery items for the workers at Tollygunge. Then Ian presents his grand surprise— six copies of *Playboy* and a large bottle of Gordon's gin. He assures me that I should be able to get at least 50 rupees for each magazine. I have a great reputation in this town! I leave Ian to his packing and, as I travel back to the hostel by bus, I calculate my new-found wealth. The magazines should bring in 300 rupees and the gin about 150. This will pay my rent for a month and provide a few decent meals as well.

Noeline and I share the toiletry items and she laughs hysterically at the magazines. 'If only Luke could see you now,' she says. Her laughter is dramatically silenced when I tell her how much I expect to get for them. Lack of money is a constant preoccupation for all of us.

During my time in Calcutta I've become adept at using the black market. My usual contact is Abdul but on this occasion he sends me to another shop that deals with these types of magazines. The men in this shop drool over the magazines but only offer 20 rupees each. I don't even bother to bargain but retrieve my booty and depart. I spend each lunch break for the next three days trying to sell these wretched publications. I'm leered at and laughed at and even develop a small following of boys interested in looking at my dirty pictures. These streets are my own backyard so there is nothing I fear here. I finally strike a bargain with a merchant who additionally offers me 100 rupees an hour for my services. Thankfully I divest myself of the troublesome magazines, rejecting his other offer with derision.

I beat a hasty retreat to No. 16 to tell Noeline of my latest adventure. She has fits of laughter and threatens to tell Sister Luke. My sense of triumph is somewhat diminished as I realise that the little rat was only offering me $10 an hour. I feel like returning to his shop and smacking him in the mouth. Although this whole business has been quite draining, Noeline and I are already making plans for our ill-gotten gains.

Noeline and I often relate tales of our escapades to Sister Luke. Noeline has a particularly Irish way of weaving a story that oft times has me wondering if we're talking about the same subject. During the bus journey to Kalighat this afternoon she again threatens to tell Luke all about my lunchtime adventures. I try to keep her in sight all afternoon but even Luke can tell from Noeline's manner that something is afoot. When she eventually corners Noeline, that Irish mouth spurts out a tale of woe about how worried for me she is because of all these strange men who keep following me. Noeline can barely keep a straight face and poor old Sister Luke goes straight into worry mode. I have overheard the lot but there is nothing I can say that will make any difference now.

The afternoon shift finally comes to a close and I try to retrieve my bag and leave quietly before I encounter Sister Luke. She is stationed at the desk, however, so there is no way of avoiding her. Concern and worry are written all over her face and as I pass by she says that she will pray for me. I could happily strangle Noeline. In the tea shop where we always meet for the obligatory post-Kalighat cuppa I find her in full flight relating my adventures to the other volunteers. By the time her performance is over even I am laughing and together we try to imagine the thoughts that will be rattling around in Sister Luke's mind tonight. Our previous experience with similar situations has produced some remarkable scenarios. For a woman who has led a reasonably sheltered life, Sister Luke can imagine almost any depravity to which a human being can sink. Hollywood scriptwriters would be proud of some of the scenarios she has imagined Noeline and I involved in. I've often found it a little disconcerting that she can so easily ascribe these bizarre activities to us. Perhaps our rather flamboyant

Left to right: Charlie, Tracey, Michelle and Noeline at a post-Kalighat
tea and smoke session

and at times completely fictitious renditions of our off-duty lifestyle have led to this confusion.

The next morning Noeline is feeling suitably remorseful, even acknowledging that she may have been a little carried away with herself and gone over the top with her story. I make her accompany me to Kalighat, as whatever happens to me this morning is going to happen to her as well. My first look at Sister Luke suggests that she has not slept all night. Before we can even put on our aprons, she is beckoning us towards the morgue. It is particularly crowded at the moment; Noeline and I perch ourselves precariously on the right-hand side while Sister Luke takes the left.

We are separated by a pine coffin, in which one of my favourite patients, Kevin, now resides. I place my feet on the coffin and steel myself for whatever is to come.

Sister Luke says, 'Girls, a pearl is something that God has given you. There will be men that will drug you and get you drunk to try and remove your pearl, but you must resist them. There will come a day when you will meet a man and fall in love and marry him. Then and only then can you relinquish your pearl.' At the end of this momentous statement she gives us both a smile and leaves. I am grateful that I had my legs to hold on to during this speech. I dare not look at Noeline and I swear to God I can feel Kevin laughing inside his coffin.

We both run from the morgue and leap up the stairs until we reach the roof and collapse into laughter. Once we have our cigarettes puffing and our choking subsides we at last dare to look at each other.

'Oh, my God. I think we just received our sex talk,' I finally manage to say. Noeline is convinced the body behind her actually moved during the great speech. It takes at least an hour before Noeline and I can pull ourselves together enough to go back downstairs and face Sister Luke again. We keep a very low profile for the rest of the day and swear to each other that this is definitely the last time we play such games.

We are pretty faithful to our commitment to refrain from juvenile pranks until one night when we decide to compose a song about our experiences here. This is what we produce through a combination of alcohol and warped senses of humour. It is sung to the tune of 'I've Never Been To Me'.

*I've been to Prem Dan and Kalighat and I spent some time
with the trots.*

I took the hand of a poorer man and just look at what I got.

*I've got scabies and lice and some parasites and some very
strange advice.*

*I talked with Mother but God love her she couldn't meet my
price.*

*I've undressed the men and washed the women and scrubbed
the floors till they shine.*

I talked with Luke about it all and heard about the pearl.

*She said it was a gem that you couldn't lend to anyone at
all. Keep it safe and in its place and never have a ball!*

 Every month Kalighat experiences a phenomenon called 'the scrub'. This common enough word is the most all-encompassing description of mayhem and sheer hard work I've ever encountered. The battle plan may sound simple: scrub and disinfect the entire interior of Kalighat. The completion time for the task is two days. Extra novices are usually called into service on these occasions.

The male ward is the first side to be attacked and those patients who are able to walk are taken to the roof. Space is made available on the female side for the rest of the patients, 'space' being a blanket on the floor. Once the patients are out of the way all the beds and mattresses are taken to the central wash area. Back out on the ward, dozens of people now proceed to crouch down on the floor and scrub every square centimetre of the space. The scrubbing equipment has a particularly Indian flavour, with shredded coconut husks used as scrubbers and a mixture of ash, lime and bleach to act as the cleaning agent. This combination, together with much back stiffness and arm wrenching, usually results in a very muddy looking floor, so we then form a line to the water tanks and pass along buckets of water to wash the whole house clean. It is always remarkable to witness a bare, fresh and, above all, clean-smelling ward. While this process is going on, another group is scrubbing the beds and mattresses and spraying them with insecticide. It is not until the afternoon that the beds are once again returned to the ward and the patients reclaim their positions. Absolutely nothing is left unscrubbed; even the dead bodies in the morgue are shifted out, so we have to wash the dishes and the beds while keeping an eye on whose corpse we are standing on or tripping over.

This may all sound quite organised and efficient but in actual practice it is one almighty nightmare. The everyday running of Kalighat must continue amid this mayhem, and feeding and caring for the patients can become manic. It is definitely not a good day for a medical emergency. Patients, sisters, volunteers and anyone within a five-kilometre radius know how to keep a low profile and their mouths shut until this military-style exercise is over.

It is a scrub day when I arrive for work this morning. I've been out of sorts and tired for several days and the last thing I feel like is this. My bad humour is noted by Sister Luke and she leaves me to look after the male patients. I've been here so long now I don't need their bed numbers to recognise each one. I spend the morning feeding and doing the dressings; every so often as I crouch down to tend to one of the men he will tell me that I'm not looking well. Having dying patients tell me I'm looking a bit sick is more than I can cope with. The regularity of the routine is the only thing that keeps me going but by the end of the morning exhaustion and another comment from a patient about me looking a little yellow has me reaching for my bag and escaping back to No. 16 and my bed.

The three flights of stairs at the Salvation Army hostel have never seemed so steep. When I finally reach my room and pause to wash my hands and face, I raise my head to the mirror and observe an extremely drawn face and two bright yellow eyes. I've never been very good about illness, having experienced so little of it, but now I decide that the correct course of action is to collapse on my bed. Being a nurse, I suffer from the common affliction known to most medical people as too much knowledge. I mentally run through every disease that includes jaundice as a symptom and come up with a lovely selection of serious or fatal conditions. Nurses always self-diagnose with something terminal. Whatever energy I had this morning has now been drained by my mental exercises so I do the only thing I can—sleep.

My illness could not have come at a worse time, with both of the other beds in the room vacant at the moment. A few days ago Noeline went to the train station to see some friends off and all their talk about beaches and holidays prompted her to just climb aboard and join them. Another volunteer returned to me with a message from Noeline which merely said, 'Gone to Goa'. The third bed in our room has been vacant for over a week now. I lie back, wallowing in an orgy of self-pity, hoping that someone will knock on my door. Salvation arrives the following evening in the form of an older Irish volunteer named Andy. My absence from three consecutive shifts at Kalighat has been noted by Sister Luke and she has dispatched Andy to investigate. By this stage I'm fully colour-coordinated and present to Andy as a bright yellow specimen from head to toe. I tell him that apart from being yellow and completely exhausted, I feel fine. He kindly fills my water bottle, replenishes my cigarette supply and prepares to report to Sister Luke in the morning.

Andy reappears the next day at lunchtime bearing a Kalighat tiffin carrier and a bag of medical supplies. The medicines are a bottle of liver tonic, vitamin B, and a list of instructions from Sister Luke. Awaiting me in the tiffin carrier is a meal of steamed fish, veg-etables and rice. The smell and sight of this concoction has me stumbling towards the bathroom. Andy has thoughtfully filled his thermos with coffee which I gratefully accept. I tell him to give the meal to the family living outside the hostel. He and I both know that he will be grilled at Kalighat tomorrow but the mere sight of food is more than I can bear. Poor Andy returns again the next day, this time bearing a green coconut of which I'm instructed to drink the water. Apparently this is a local treatment for jaundice. He is also armed with instructions to ascertain my dietary preferences. The return of an empty tiffin car-rier and a sheepish Andy did not fool Sister Luke. Four days without food has produced the beginnings of an appetite and somewhat wistfully I write down roast beef and tomato toasted sandwiches. Andy shakes his head in amazement and once again prepares to act as the conduit between 'two impossible women'.

By the morning of the fifth day I'm sick to death of the sight of my room and judge that I can summon up enough energy to make it to the local coffee shop. This proves to be a more taxing journey than I had anticipated and it's with an enormous sense of relief that I collapse onto a bench inside the café. My arrival has not impressed the boys that run this establishment; they mutter something about yellow not being good for business. I am a long-time customer here and have dispensed medical advice and supplies to all of them so, after a short rest, two of the lads help me back to my room and promise to deliver coffee on a regular basis to No. 16. God, now I know how the lepers feel! I sleep soundly for a few hours and wake to find Andy and his tiffin carrier in the room once again. He has a wicked grin on his face as I open the container. The first compartment is filled with several pieces of toast, the second with two tomatoes and the third with a dozen slices of beef. I can't believe she really did it. I'm not allowed any fat so I make a sandwich with the dry toast, beef and tomato and for the first time in five days feel my stomach accept food without protest. It's like a little bit of heaven. The Irish must have a built-in beef detector because within hours of my food arriving two of the village girls turn up and help me to empty my container ready for its return to Kalighat.

Over the coming days I receive my tiffin carrier from one of the volunteers and each day there is beef or meat of some description. One memorable meal even had prawns as well as all the usual goodies. I have become amazingly popular during this period and the Irish girls, as well as other volunteers, call in each afternoon to enquire after my health and to help empty whatever is left in the tiffin carrier.

After lying idle for over a week I decide to go out to Kalighat for Sunday mass. I catch the bus and slowly walk towards Kalighat. It's not until I'm inside that this exertion catches up with me and I nearly faint. The only response I receive for my rather heroic gesture is a sound tongue-lashing from Sister Luke, who bundles me into a taxi as soon as mass is over, instructing Andy to take me home. I'm also told not to come back for another two weeks. And here I was thinking I was indispensable. Talk about kicking a person when they're down. The up-side to all this is that my illness has landed holiday-maker Noeline in Sister Luke's bad books. She returns a few days later and is suitably impressed by my new colour. When she returns to Kalighat, Sister Luke gives her a bucketing for not being here when needed. I tell her that it is only retribution for the number of times that she's landed me in it at Kalighat. The meals continue to arrive, so Noeline and I live like kings. The really horrible part about having hepatitis is that alcohol is strictly forbidden.

I finally return to normal colour, and two and a half weeks after my collapse I return to Kalighat and slowly get back into my normal routine. I've been extremely lucky during my time in India and, apart from this hepatitis, have only had scabies and lice, a short burst of dysentery and a carbuncle. Sister Luke continues to feed me for another three weeks and then stops. I'm now pronounced recovered and will have to fend for myself again.

 There comes a time when you finally realise you have been in Calcutta too long. Today has been such a moment for me. Travelling back on the bus from Kalighat at lunchtime, I think nothing of it when the bus abruptly stops mid-journey and we are all told to get off. I even join my fellow commuters in abusing the conductor and demanding my money back. I eventually shrug my shoulders and walk the length of Chowringhee, pausing only to buy my usual luncheon fare of an egg roll from a street vendor. I turn into Sudder Street, then the Sally Army hostel, go up the stairs and, upon reaching my room, set my alarm clock for 2.30 and gratefully fall asleep. This is my everyday routine. I wake, wash and go down to the Blue Sky Café for coffee. The roller door of the cafe is three-quarters shut but this fails to make much impression on my brain and I simply scurry under the bottom. I order a half-glass of coffee and only then notice that the place is nearly empty and the boys very agitated. They are glued to the radio and at 2.50 the newsreader announces that Indira Gandhi has been assassinated. With this announcement I'm ushered out of the shop and its shutter is firmly closed down.

All along Sudder Street this same thing is being repeated.

As it is almost time to return to Kalighat I make my way to Chowringhee. Here I discover that all transport has suddenly ceased. Millions of people are trying to make their way home and all of them seem to be out on the street. My main philosophy—if you can't beat them, join them—seems appropriate to this occasion and I join the human wave going in the Kalighat direction. It is quite a peaceful crowd and although not overly boisterous, certainly not morose. There is no sign of unrest until I pass by the Sikh area on Hazra Road. Here there are signs that shops and homes have been attacked, and a car is burning in the street. I continue on with the crowd and eventually make it to Kalighat without incident. I discover that walking to Kalighat has only taken five minutes longer than the bus.

Sister Luke is furious that I am even here and gives me a long lecture on my stupidity. According to her, the streets are alive with violence and the whole place is about to explode. God only knows where she gets all this information from. Living in a convent tends to magnify the dangers of everyday living in Calcutta. Apparently we have now entered a period of three days of mourning for Indira Gandhi. Everything must come to a stop with the exception of ambulances and the emergency services such as the Missionaries of Charity. I catch a lift back to the Mother House and walk home from there. Along the way we see the odd bus or car burning brightly in the night. It has always amazed me that when people wish to demonstrate their anger in Calcutta they invariably pick on some form of vehicle to set on fire.

The only real difficulties that Noeline and I encounter are finding somewhere to eat and a place to buy cigarettes. As we know virtually every eating establishment in our vicinity, we keep trying back doors until one Chinese restaurant lets us in. There are also the dozens of street children that inform us of what can be bought and where to get it. The streets are certainly much quieter and it is a marvellous opportunity to observe Calcutta minus the millions of people and the endless activity. Noeline and I spend the next morning wandering the streets, half-hoping to come across some action, but a couple of hours produces nothing but boredom. We decide to walk out to Kalighat for the afternoon session. Sister Luke finds it hard to believe our reports that there is no violence or mayhem but as we are so short-staffed thoughts of the outside world are soon replaced with the work at hand. I spend the next two days walking to and from Kalighat and never experience any difficulties. It is actually quite pleasant and gives a measure of time for thought and introspection.

Eventually the mourning period is over and Calcutta blasts back into life. Over breakfast I read the local paper and according to their reports the whole city has been racked with violence. The army has even been called out and a curfew has been in place. One of the bus casualties is displayed prominently on the front page. Thank God for the media or I would never have known what an exciting time I had just lived through. I had better write to my mother and reassure her that her only daughter is alive and well in the midst of all this excitement.

*

Several weeks later my life has fallen back into the same old routines. We had a party in our room last night and as the alarm clock thunders in my head I rise and stagger towards the bathroom. On my journey I collect an empty bottle with my toe and, as I jump around in agony, discover a message under the bottle. It reads, 'Tressy, Mother Teresa wants to see you this morning.' I bash Noeline on my way past her bed and try to clear my head under the shower. Noeline is still lying in the same position when I return. Following the pattern of several months, I give her another violent shake and depart for my breakfast.

While I am savouring the delights of an omelette and hot tea, Noeline turns up and orders coffee and a paratha. I tell her that I don't think her joke is very funny and she just looks at me like I'm stupid. We are both running on reduced brain cells this morning. When I tell her about the note, she pleads total innocence. I don't believe her for a minute. It is not until a French volunteer named Bridget stops by and asks me if I received her note that the reality of the situation finally hits me. She is a particularly honest individual and is even planning to join the Missionaries of Charity herself. Noeline roars with laughter as my face turns pale. She is in her element, suggesting every possible reason for my summons, from being hijacked into the convent to being thrown out of the country. Neither my stomach nor head have been feeling particularly bright this morning and now I decide to return to my room and die. Noeline won't let me out of her sight and continues to badger me about going to the Mother House. Eventually I cave in and decide to go down and see what's happening. Noeline escorts me to the door and then informs me that she will now pop out to Kalighat and let Sister Luke know the latest developments. I can hear her snorting laughter as she walks down the lane. My head feels like it is about to explode.

I inform one of the sisters at the Mother House that I have received a message to see Mother Teresa here this morning and then wait on one of the benches until they can find out what's going on. Eventually I'm escorted upstairs and Mother is waiting outside the chapel. She asks me what I want and I remind her that it is she who has called me here. After a few moments of confusion we both sit on a bench and she questions me about my time here in Calcutta. It is a most natural conversation and, as I relax, my mouth gets carried away with itself yet again.

Warming to my topic, I decide to let Mother know where I think she can improve things. I start by telling her that she is the second most powerful person in the Catholic Church today and with that power she should be out there demanding change and attacking the causes of poverty. I'm just getting into my stride when she interrupts and asks me what I would want her to do for me if I were lying in a gutter, dying and hungry. Would I like her to pick me up or to find the department or institution responsible for my wellbeing? Of course I say that I would wish to be picked up. She then tells me that years ago God told her to help the poorest of the poor in the manner that she is doing and until she receives other directives that is what she will continue to do. Her final message to me is that when I go home I should go to Katherine and work with the Aborigines. She gives me a blessing and that's that.

It is not until I'm standing in the bus on the way to Kalighat that the reality of the whole experience finally hits home. I shouldn't be allowed out on my own. To think that I've had the cheek to tell Mother Teresa how to run her affairs! It is obvious that whatever the message under the bottle meant this morning it certainly wasn't divine intervention. When I finally reach Kalighat, Sister Luke is brimming with joy and anxious to hear all about my talk with Mother. I grab Noeline and we head for the roof. Her raucous laughter can be heard for miles as I describe my meeting with Mother. I wish I'd stayed in bed this morning. I have to tell Luke something and eventually just say that Mother said I should go home and work with the Aborigines. Needless to say, this is not the news she has been praying for all these years.

 Eventually December comes around and those of us with temporary resident's permits must leave the country. I've been in India for eighteen months this time. There have been moments when it has seemed like an eternity, others when it has felt like only a matter of days. My ever-precarious finances are just about exhausted and it is time I returned home. Learning from my previous experience of returning to the family home, I decide to divest myself of most of my worldly goods before my mother can put a match to them. All my perfectly wearable Indian clothes of 1981 ended up in a bonfire that my mother started as her contribution to infection control. I sell my jeans to Noeline and my backpack and cassette radio in the market. While emptying my backpack I come across my Vegemite jar full of marijuana. Noeline has never experienced the delights of the dreaded weed and as I'm more than likely going to hell in a handbasket, I decide that corrupting one more soul won't make any difference. Unfortunately Noeline experienced none of the pleasures of being high as the sheer tension of her illicit act made her violently ill.

I decide to return home for Christmas. Noeline is going to try her luck in Bombay and hopes to extend her visa there. Leaving this time is very different from my last experience. I'm physically and emotionally drained and it feels right to be leaving. I've just been going through the motions lately and the world around me has started to fade. My batteries need a lengthy recharge. I have recovered from the yellow peril but have failed to gain much weight. At least this will garner some sympathy when I return home. My previous return only produced amusement from my family and friends, who kindly pointed out that I was the only person alive to gain weight in India!

Sister Luke is still under the mistaken impression that I have a vocation and assures me that I'll be back again one day. Kalighat is a place that gets under your skin and every time you scratch, it brings back memories. The volunteers throw a party on the roof of the hostel and we spend the night drinking and telling old war stories. The volunteer community is as diverse in theology as it is in nationality, stretching from the deeply religious through varying degrees of faith all the way to atheist. The remarkable thing about all of us is that we are so completely ordinary. Anyone can come here and feel really good about themselves just by spooning food into someone's mouth. When we return to our homes, we keep this secret to ourselves. Any attempt to share this simple truth with others in Western countries is met with incomprehension and disbelief. This night, however, we drink and recount some of the more memorable and bizarre happenings of the past year.

I had forgotten all about last Easter when Sister Luke went all out in her efforts to guide her many straying volunteers back to the Catholic Church. She is always fervent in her work for God and considers the volunteers a challenge to be overcome. She was horrified when she discovered just before Easter that Marc, a French vet, hadn't been to confession for over twelve years. A quick questioning of the other volunteers uncovered four others with similar histories. I was among that group. With a mixture of browbeating and bribery she had us all agreeing to attend confession before Easter. We considered this an easy thing to promise as she would never know one way or the other. Much to our surprise, a beaming Sister Luke then informed us she had found a priest who would be at Kalighat within the hour. The old Jesuit turned up and a pseudo confessional was arranged at the end of the female ward. We trouped in, one after the other, and by the time the priest reappeared he was looking decidedly pale. I don't know what the others told him but I gave him my views on confession and he just shook his head. Sister Luke was happy and that was all that mattered.

*

We make it to the airport the next day by good luck rather than good management. Somewhere along the way I lose my resident's permit, so when I try to go through customs, they refuse me. I'm not in the greatest of conditions and when I tell them that I don't want to leave anyway, they are even more perplexed.

My name must be on a list somewhere, because they eventually tell me I must go and escort me out to the plane.

It is so typically Calcutta—drama right to the end.

PART THREE

New Beginnings
Port Keats, Northern Territory,
May 1985 October 1988

 Restless again, and ready to take another step out into the great unknown. I've been home for four months now and have decided to rejoin the work force. My younger brother, Richard of the religious bent, has found an advertisement for a nurse to work in the Northern Territory and the only obstacle as far as I can see is that the employers are Catholic missions. I seem destined to remain within the fold of the church.

I apply for the position and receive a phone call from one of the sisters up there. Apparently my written résumé went over quite well. Histories always look so nice and uncomplicated on paper that I must appear a perfect candidate for the missionary field. God help them when they finally meet the flesh and blood version. Sister Patricia tells me all about an Aboriginal settlement called Port Keats. At first I thought she said Port Quiche but hoped that I was wrong. It has a population of 1300 and a clinic with two nursing sisters and one lay nurse. She describes the basic work involved, saying that with my experience I'll have no trouble at all. I have never been known for pondering major life decisions for very long, so I tell her it sounds okay and I'll take the position.

Mum and I spend the next few days trying to find a map of Australia with Port Keats marked on it. Eventually we hit pay dirt and discover it on the western coast of the Northern Territory facing the Joseph Bonaparte Gulf. There is nothing else on the map for hundreds of kilometres. Before any serious second thoughts can set in, a woman from Catholic Missions calls and tells me all about the pay and conditions. I will receive $20 000 a year, and a subsidised flat is also provided. The flat is equipped with cutlery, crockery, linen and all essentials, so all I need to buy are some blue uniforms. I cringe at the thought of uniforms all over again. I nearly fall off the chair when this woman asks me if, given my history as a volunteer, I would like to work as a lay missionary and only accept living expenses? God, are they in for a shock. I quickly inform this lady that I desperately need a salary as I'm stone motherless broke. This response eventually drives the message home. She asks when I'll be arriving and I tell her not until they send a ticket.

In Darwin I am met by one of the workers at Catholic Missions who drives me into town. Estelle is responsible for staff as well as the mountain of paperwork that running this organisation requires. She informs me that I need to open a Commonwealth Bank account so that I may receive my wages, and that I should purchase a few groceries while in town. Apparently I am due to fly out to Port Keats in the morning. I'm bundled into another car, driven to the local business district and left to my own devices.

The girl in the bank who processes my application recoils in horror when she reads that I'm going to Port Keats. According to her it is a terrible place in which I'm likely to be murdered. I begin to wish I could acquire the knack of learning from experience. Why don't I do a little more homework before setting out on these adventures? Too late now. I sort out a bank account, do a little grocery shopping and then make my way back to Catholic Missions. I sit in my little room and wonder, not for the first time in my life, if I am completely sane.

In an effort to make me feel at home, Estelle announces that she will drop me out at the Missionaries of Charity so that I can visit with the sisters. This notion robs me of speech and I simply follow the leader. I seem destined to be around nuns wherever I go. I am dropped off at the front gate and before I have even introduced myself to all the sisters I'm bundled into another van and driven several blocks away to one of their shelters. God only knows who they think I am.

After we have disembarked I'm handed an apron and directed towards the kitchen. Apparently the Missionaries of Charity are the same the world over. Anyone foolish enough to stand in front of them gets handed an apron and put to work. As I peel and cut potatoes, I learn that we are feeding some of the local Aborigines and a few derelicts. When the cooking is completed, a few people straggle in to the shelter. This being a Missionaries of Charity operation, economy is the guiding principle. Each person receives a meal of sausages, mashed potato and peas with a buttered bread roll. If they wish to take the food away, the whole concoction is spooned into an old plastic bag for convenient transportation. What the food looks and tastes like when the lucky recipients reach their destinations I dread to think. This activity and talk with the sisters at least keeps my mind from wondering what I will face tomorrow.

I spend a very restless evening and night thinking about Port Keats. It dawns on me that I have never met an Aborigine in my life. I know nothing about their culture or spiritual beliefs. All I really know about the Aboriginal race is what I've seen on television and I have grown quite sceptical about the media over the years. I have been employed for my nursing experience and nobody has really mentioned anything about cultural or spiritual problems that may exist. My time in India has at least taught me respect for other religions and cultures and the importance of these in people's lives. The one thing I do know for sure about Port Keats is that it is a 'dry' settlement. No alcohol is allowed. This time I am really serious about turning over a new leaf. I wonder how many leaves are left on my particular tree.

I rise early in the morning to catch a lift with the Catholic Missions bus out to the airport. My plane this time is a twelve-seater, twin-engine machine. I haven't had much experience with small planes except for a very brief interlude while I was on night duty during my nurses' training. Night duty tends to warp the brain and as a result I was somehow talked into going parachuting. I only ever had two jumps and I am still amazed to have survived. This plane does not come equipped with parachutes, so I will be saved that experience again. There are several other passengers, all of them Aboriginal. We greet each other with a nod and that is the extent of conversation.

As the plane takes off and heads out over the bush I begin to wonder why I always seem to fly in to my new adventures. I'm always dropping out of the sky into a completely foreign environment.

We land at Daly River and I'm quite impressed with what I've seen from the air of this lovely, lush, community. Our next stop is at Palumpa cattle station, which is only a tiny group of buildings in the middle of nowhere. As we circle Port Keats my eyes devour the layout of the place. There are a few hundred homes and buildings set amid the red earth. The lush green tropical paradise that I've been expecting is nowhere to be seen. There is also no evidence of any beaches or coastal vegetation. My mental balloon has been well and truly exploded this time.

I step down from the plane and I'm greeted by Sister Pauline, the sister in charge of the clinic. She eyes my bag and asks if this is all the luggage I've brought. I look with apprehension at my battered little bag, veteran of my first Indian adventure, and wonder what else I could possibly need here. We climb aboard a Landcruiser troop carrier with 'Ambulance' written on its side and Sister Pauline drives down the main dry, dusty road pointing out buildings of interest as we go. As she pulls into the clinic area it suddenly strikes me that I've never seen people as black as this before. The Aborigines gathered outside and inside the clinic are all the colour of charcoal. I eventually close my gaping mouth and manage to shuffle my way through dozens of introductions. Sister Pauline then takes me down to the nurses' quarters and I'm given the last of the three flats. Maria, the other nurse, occupies the first flat and the second is kept for visiting medical staff. My mouth is gaping once more as I view my new accommodation. It is a low brick building with extended roofing on either side to minimise the effects of the sun. My flat contains a small bedroom with airconditioning and a lounge room furnished with a table, chairs and two armchairs. There is a small kitchen with stove, fridge and freezer and another room with the toilet and shower. To me it seems like luxury on a grand scale in comparison to No. 16 at the Salvation Army hostel in Calcutta. Sister Pauline is already scratching her head over her latest employee and leaves me to settle in. It is going to take me a while to stop comparing everything here to Calcutta.

 The following day I'm given an introduction to the main clinic. This consists of a large waiting area with bench seats. Branching off this main room are two treatment rooms, with a separate room used for medication and equipment storage. At the far end there are the toilet and shower facilities. Overhead fans swirl in a fruitless effort to lighten the humid atmosphere. At least the climate is familiar to me. The clinic and its operation is as modern and well-equipped as you would find anywhere in Australia. Standing here in my clean new uniform, I suddenly feel completely out of place and unsure of my ability to work in a structured and accountable institution.

My clinic tour is fairly brief, as Sister Pauline is constantly being called to attend to various patients. I spend the morning trying to familiarise myself with the contents of the numerous cupboards and drawers. I recoil in horror when I discover the paper cabinet and I am confronted by dozens of different coloured pages that somehow all combine to make up a person's chart. The bane of every nurse's existence is paperwork and I feel sorely tempted to torch this mountainous supply. The other significant piece of

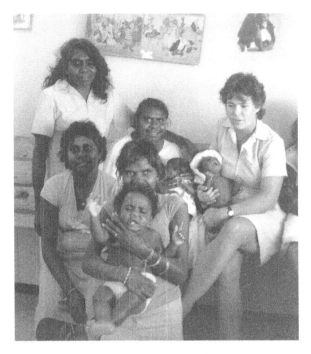

Tracey with the Port Keats health workers *(clockwise from top)*:
Lillian, Philippine, Ethelreda and Sabrina

equipment in the main room is the two-way radio. This is our link to Darwin and medical help. At least one of my fantasies has come true.

There is another, smaller, clinic near the main shop and council building. This is called the baby clinic and caters for the 0–5-year-old population. Sister Lee and Maria work here alongside five of the Aboriginal health workers. There are another five health workers in the main clinic.

One of my surprises this morning is to discover that all the Aborigines speak another language. This is called Murringhpatha and is the language of this area. I will definitely have to do a little study of Aboriginal history and culture if I'm ever going to come up to speed here. Fortunately the locals are multilingual and communication in English is not nearly as difficult as in India. Doubts about my suitability for this job are starting to multiply. Sick babies scare me to death. I wish I were more qualified and experienced in the areas in which I am obviously going to be working.

Sister Pauline gives me a tour of the settlement. The actual beaches are several kilometres away and Port Keats' access to the sea is via the landing and a creek through the mangroves, appropriately enough called Sandfly Creek. The site of the community has been chosen for its accessibility to fresh water rather than for aesthetic reasons. The roads are all unpaved, so a cloud of dust follows us and settles wherever it can. Now I realise why everything has a dull red appearance. As we drive around, Sister Pauline explains that each area has a name that roughly equates with the different tribes living there. The main names are top camp, middle camp, bottom camp, creek camp, Dumoo camp. To my very simple mind it seems like a mini-suburb system. The housing varies from new besser-block homes to dozens of tiny boxes which, I am informed, are called demountables. These are rectangular boxes, made of tin, with a door and a couple of windows. The other striking feature of my tour is the number of plastic bags and other rubbish that swirls about in the ever-present dust. I can't stop myself from thinking that some little Indian could make a nice living out of this lot.

Eventually my first day is over. I've been introduced to so many people that I'll never remember any of their names. Maria and I sit down with a coffee and she does her best to assure me that I will fit in just fine. She gives me an overview of the general illnesses encountered and the treatments that take place at the clinic and once she has calmed my fears on this score she tries to educate my empty head on the subject of the Aboriginal people of Port Keats. Maria is from Emerald in Queensland and has been working here for the last eighteen months. She is of slight build with blonde hair which certainly makes her a novelty in this environment. Maria is relieved to finally have another nurse around and as we both discover a similar sense of irreverent humour, we become firm friends.

We are interrupted by a few of the health workers and several children. Apparently they are all frequent visitors to Maria's flat. Once everyone has a drink they settle down to their prime objective, which is to find out all about me. It is a joyous surprise to find that we're all on the same mission, except from different sides. When I explain that I've been working in India for the last few years they are most distressed and anxious to know if they can 'send any tucker to dem hungry ones'? The genuine warmth and sincerity of this offer makes me feel for the first time that I will eventually grow to love it here.

It is Friday night and Maria takes me to a party that the teachers are having. There are about eighty white people living in Port Keats and their occupations are varied—teachers, nurses, mechanics, plumbers, builders, electricians, storekeepers, bank tellers, post office workers. As I enter the house where the party is in progress I'm assailed by a sense of deja vu and remember the Marine House in Calcutta. Dozens of people are happily dancing and drinking beer and generally having a wild old time. I feel my nice new leaf start to wither once again. Maria explains that although Port Keats is a dry settlement they have a club which operates six nights a week from 5.00 p.m. to 6.30 p.m. and each member is allowed to buy four cans of beer. White people are allowed to apply for a liquor licence and, once granted, can buy and keep alcohol in their homes. I manage to survive the evening without so much as a drop of beer, although the sight of all those cold cans on such a warm and sticky evening is very tempting.

On Sunday Maria takes me out bush. This entails climbing onto the back of a four-wheel drive ute and driving around the camp, stopping at various houses until the back is filled with people and off we go. We drive along dirt tracks until we reach the sea, whereupon everybody seems to disappear in different directions. They are all searching for food. I'm completely out of my depth and happily join Maria and Bill (a builder) in gathering firewood for the billy and a nice cup of tea.

I spent all the school holidays of my youth on my uncle's farm in Queensland and I have a great love for the Australian bush. It doesn't scare me and I can only hope that once I've started to feel at home here the Aborigines will show me more of this country. The biggest tragedy of the day is to be sitting on this pristine white beach and unable to swim. On the journey out here Maria and my other companions started to list the predators inhabiting the local waters. I made them stop after crocodiles, sharks and box jelly fish. The kids thought it a great joke and continued naming all sorts of animals until I held my hands over my ears. It seemed everyone had a disaster story to relate, just in case the litany of man-eaters failed to make an impression. I have finally found my tropical paradise, only to have it snatched away again.

On Monday Sister Pauline informs me that I am to work with Sister Lee and Maria in the baby clinic. The mere thought of this fills me with terror. My experience with children is non-existent and their size and frailty frighten me.

I proceed to the baby clinic and am immediately assailed by the piercing sound of several babies crying. The baby clinic is a small besser-block building with a metal grille and gate acting as the front wall. A large bench runs along the inside of the front grille, bearing a set of scales on which each baby and child is weighed before entering the main clinic area. The clinic consists of a large room with benches at either end, a refrigerator, two sinks, bench and cupboard space. There is a stainless steel treatment trolley and a small wooden desk. This is the principal work area for the clinic, with a further two rooms on the right-hand side of the building comprising a storeroom, toilet and tea room. Maria explains the general workings of the clinic and I spend the morning observing the diagnosis and treatment given to the many dozens of children brought in by their mothers. I spend every spare moment of the following week reading all the medical textbooks in the clinic until, through a process of study and observation, I eventually feel competent to attend these little creatures.

By the end of my first full week I'm starting to feel that I will enjoy my time here. The Aboriginal health workers are the mainstay of the place and they are very patient in explaining various dos and don'ts of their culture. They are basically a very shy people but extremely good humoured, and laughter is the most dominant sound heard around the place.

My third weekend here brings the fearful and timid side of Port Keats' inhabitants to the surface as the word is spread that a cyclone is coming our way. Tracey is a very unfortunate name to possess in cyclone territory, as it reminds everybody of the cyclone that destroyed Darwin in 1974. Even more frightening for some of the Port Keats residents is the fact that they were in Darwin when this cyclone hit. Maria and I haven't heard anything officially about it yet, but Maria tells me that the Aborigines always know what's going on before anybody else does.

Saturday night, and Sister Pauline calls us all to the clinic and informs us that the cyclone is expected to hit that night. Apparently the clinic is cyclone-proof and contains several boxes sent out each year from Darwin as the cyclone survival kits. She then tells us that we will each go to different shelters. This is to maximise the chances of survival of the nurses to care for the injured, just in case one or more of the shelters are destroyed! My feelings of goodwill are quickly starting to evaporate. Guided by some divine inspiration, Sister Pauline directs me to the police station and jail. I've only been here three weeks and already she has me worked out.

I join about a dozen of the white community in the police station while a hundred or more Aborigines congregate in the courthouse and jail area. The best part about my position is having the police radio, which generates a great sense of excitement. The only obvious physical aspects of the cyclone are the strong winds and torrential rain. This doesn't appear terribly severe but strong enough to lift loose iron sheeting and rock some of the more flimsy buildings around the place. As the night wears on and the excitement is still bubbling, the policeman's wife, Christine, and I act as weather observers for the meteorological bureau in Darwin. We monitor the radio and they ask us to report wind direction and speed. This puts us in something of a dilemma as we have no instruments to accurately record this information. Lance, the policeman in charge, takes us outside and by shining a heavy duty torch on the trees tells us how to judge the wind direction. We collapse in laughter as we both confess to having no idea which way is north or south. His patience and humour are not in large supply tonight and with a few hurried instructions he leaves us to our task and continues his, which is to make sure that everybody in Port Keats has found shelter. Once Christine and I are confident that north lies at the landing end of the main street we feel that we have finally worked out the wind direction but are at a loss to judge speed. We don't like to feel left out, so we just use the last speed from the weather bureau and drop it 20 kilometres. This process continues for hours, and as the novelty begins to wear off we all become anxious to return to our beds. While the wind and rain has certainly been strong, it has had little effect on the brick buildings and only the tin shacks and a few trees have been damaged. We ask the meteorological bureau if we can all go home but are informed that our high winds will have to drop before that will be allowed. Christine and I realise that our over-zealous reporting is contributing to our discomfort and over the coming hour adjust our wind speed recording to enable us to go home.

It has certainly been a night with a difference and I've got to know some of the other residents here quite well. Christine and Lance have been here about a year and in the Territory around ten years. From Christine I learn about the violence and problems affecting Port Keats. It seems that many in the white community see this place as hardship duty and their many years in the north have hardened their attitudes towards the Aborigines and their problems. She says little that is positive to add to my meagre knowledge of this place. This latest adventure of mine could prove just as crazy as my last.

THIRTY-EIGHT

During the following weeks I gradually get myself organised. The longer I spend in the baby clinic the more confident I become. The most frustrating part about treating babies and small children is their inability to communicate. I must rely more than usual on my own observations and assessment of their conditions. One amazing statistic that I have learnt here is that the under-fives number 205 in a population of only 1300. The most common ailments are chest infections, diarrhoea and vomiting, malnutrition, anaemia, ear infections and skin infections. The contributing factors that cause these diseases are as diverse as the illnesses themselves. When I first went to India I thought I had all the answers, only to learn that the longer I stayed there the less I knew. I have the same problems here in Port Keats. Unfortunately there are never simple answers to any of these problems and I've got a lot to learn before I'll be able to contribute to any solution.

The people of Port Keats have never lived anywhere else and the first white people, Catholic missionaries, only arrived here fifty years ago. When the mission was established the seven tribes living in the area were placed together. The bringing together of all these tribes to live in Murringhpatha country has created problems ever since. Each tribe has its own particular language, laws and customs, and the enmity between the different groups often has its roots in centuries-old taboos. I do not pretend to understand much about the traditional way of life for these people but slowly the health workers and patients try to steer me along a path where at the very least I'll learn how not to give offence. My discoveries to date are that eye contact is considered to be rude, directions are usually given via a pursing of the lips and head movement, and numbers are basically irrelevant. The number business astonishes me. The general description of distance is anything from 'short one' to 'long way', the actual length depending on the amount of emphasis placed on the word long. When describing things the usual terms for size are 'little bit' or 'big mobs'. Needless to say, the Western concept of time is quite alien to the locals. This is all a difficult adjustment for the number-obsessed Western mind.

Another surprising observation about Port Keats is that the pace of life here is even slower than in India. We work a normal eight-hour day in the clinic, but apart from this the whole environment is very laid back. The outside world barely impinges on us. Maria has a television which receives ABC programs but there is no radio, and newspapers always arrive several days out of date. Slowly the outside world starts to recede and all the small happenings of Port Keats take on greater significance. It's amazing to think that twelve months ago I was living in a city with nine million people and now I'm living with 1300.

The sense of isolation is reinforced by our geographical position. We are only 350 kilometres from Darwin but this is at least a six and a half hour road journey. There is an air service three mornings a week, and once a month a barge makes its way up the creek to the landing. The barge is the only totally reliable contact with the outside world, as the roads and landing strip become waterlogged during the wet season. There are only two distinct seasons here, the dry and the wet, each lasting for about six months.

This type of insular community tends to bond people together. The 'whitefellas' socialise together, regardless of background, and there is usually a gathering of all the white people at least once a month. I have convinced Maria that we should both get alcohol permits and, as usual, I'm in the middle of most parties that happen here.

The other important forms of entertainment are cards and fishing. Maria has taught me how to play Five Hundred and we play at least twice a week. Fishing is the other must-do entertainment and the local store provides plastic hand-reels and other bits and pieces. The waters up here are so full of fish that the most basic equipment will provide a bountiful catch. Maria and I have bought a small four-wheel drive vehicle and we like to spend at least one day of the weekend with the health workers out bush. I ask Lillian to take me crabbing with them and after much discussion with the other women, who appear to

Tracey and catch, Port Keats

express doubts about my capabilities, they finally relent and allow me to accompany them.

We enter a mangrove and the further in we wade, the more the mud becomes like quicksand. I stick to Lillian like glue, trying as hard as I can to keep up with her and not cause any embarrassment. The humiliating part of the ordeal is that as we go along Lillian is trying to teach me some basic bush skills. She points out crab tracks to me. I stare like a blind person at an indecipherable sea of mud. I'll be happy just to get out of this sweat box alive, but Lillian follows the tracks as if they are fluorescent signs and within minutes has captured a large mud crab. Lillian continues to point out various landmarks but it's still just one big jungle of mangrove roots and mud to me. A few hours later we stumble back onto solid ground, me covered in mud from head to toe. Much to my amazement the other women congratulate me, as though I've passed through some rite of passage. They tell me that I can come with them again. Although this is the furthest thought from my mind, I have the wit to accept gratefully. During the following weeks and months my skills improve, to the stage where I am able to recognise parts of the mangroves and over-come my fear of drowning in mud, but the recognition of crab tracks is still way beyond me. My most embarrassing, yet triumphant, moment comes when I stop for a smoke on a mangrove root and, as I move to stand up again, I land on a crab. I quickly remove its claws and place it in my empty bag, return-ing to the other women like the last of the great white hunters. After this fluke, my fame as a skilled crab hunter spreads throughout the community.

A few months after I arrive, Sister Pauline is trans-ferred back to Darwin, so Sister Lee and Maria take over the running of the main clinic. This leaves me in charge of the four health workers at the baby clinic. I have a nervous attack, envisaging dozens of babies dying due to my incompetence. Responsibility is a ter-rifying load to carry.

As I assume control of my little clinic I begin to understand why so many people have been accused of paternalism when dealing with the Aboriginal people. My initial response to disease of any kind is usually anger. I hate seeing the weak, vulnerable and poor always suffering the worst. I can become quite volatile when fighting for my patients and consider all 205 children in Port Keats to be my personal responsibility. This attitude is not conducive to mental health but no-one has ever accused me of being totally sane.

The set-up in the baby clinic is designed to maximise the child's chance of a healthy start in life. We try to weigh all the babies at least once a week, and older children once a month. Each child is entered into the immunisation book the moment he or she returns from hospital and all due immunisations appear on our whiteboard each month, to be erased only when completed. We are justly proud of a 98 per cent immunisation coverage.

The biggest obstacles to good health in this community are nutritional and environmental. Poor housing and overcrowding, together with poor hygiene and a reliance on basic Western food such as flour, tea and sugar, combine to exacerbate any outbreak of disease. All the common acute diseases of childhood—diarrhoea and vomiting, chest infection and earaches—become chronic, and further weaken the child's immune system. We heroically treat all these conditions with the best that modern medicine can provide, but unfortunately this makes little impression in the long run. The lack of coordination in the application of government resources often has me wanting to tear my hair out. We run mass deworming programs while the main causes of these parasites, such as the diseased dogs, broken sewerage pipes and inadequate garbage disposal, await their turn on the bureaucratic merry-go-round. Each and every health problem has multiple corresponding infrastructure and managerial roots. The day these are ever acknowledged and remedied will be a miracle for Aboriginal health.

The health workers' names are Lillian, Phillipine, Gerada and Lucia. They have all seen nurses and nuns come and go and are quite philosophical about the constant change. They are very quiet, and only Lillian has the confidence to show me what to do and teach me new ways. Lillian is in her late forties and is an elder in this community. In her early years she joined the Sisters of Our Lady of the Sacred Heart but, like several of her contemporaries, found the religious life incompatible with her Aboriginal culture. As a health worker and 'aunty' she has raised dozens of children in this community. Whenever a difficult case arises and a caring responsible person is required, everyone automatically thinks of Lillian. I consider myself lucky to call her friend and have her guide me through this experience. On the whole the Aboriginal women are very shy and reluctant to answer questions. My whole demeanour and style of living has given rise to much gossip in this community. At least I draw some laughs from them in the baby clinic as we all become accustomed to each other's personalities. I have learnt two Murringhpatha phrases. These describe 'cracked in the head' and 'no brain'! I wonder if they are telling me something.

 I have been at Port Keats for five months now but it feels like I've been here forever. The big news is that my mother is coming to visit. I spend days cleaning my flat and trying to add a few home-like touches. My surroundings don't often have an impact on me but my mother notices everything. I ask Maria to give my place the once-over; when she says it's fine I cease cleaning but continue worrying. I fly to Darwin and book into a hostel that the teachers have told me about. I borrow an old Landcruiser truck when my mother's plane is due and go out to meet her.

When I see my mother coming towards me from the plane I'm thrilled that she has finally found the opportunity to see what I'm doing with my life. She is immaculately dressed and gives my outfit the silent negative appraisal. As usual I'm dressed in shorts, T-shirt and thongs, fashion never having found space in my life. Her jaw drops when she sees the Landcruiser and she asks me how to climb into it.

Things go from bad to worse. I drive us to the hostel and Mum stares in disbelief when I announce that this is where we are staying the night. I try to lighten the atmosphere by informing her that it used to be the nurses' quarters and she can pretend to be back in her old training days. The rooms are clean and more than adequate by my standards, but the communal bathroom and the multi-racial inhabitants almost have my mother returning to the airport.

I know my mother loves me but I can't help feeling that she wishes I possessed a few more feminine and social graces. I bundle her into the truck again and we set off for the shops. I buy hundreds of dollars' worth of groceries and consign most of these to be transported to Port Keats on the next barge. Leaving Mum outside the supermarket I go to collect the truck and suddenly realise I have no idea where I left it. Unfortunately Landcruisers are as common as mud round here. This is my first trip back to Darwin since I arrived so I'm as much a novice here as my mother. One hour later I strike it lucky and return to collect a very confused and worried mother.

We board the little plane for Port Keats in the morning. Mum loses a few more shades of colour and spends the journey in silent prayer, as I try valiantly to point out the different areas we are flying over. There is rather a large crowd waiting at the airstrip and, as we gather our luggage, Mum is surrounded by children eager to welcome Tracey's mother and guide her towards the ambulance. I make brief introductions and suddenly we're in the back of the ambulance along with twenty others, driving towards the clinic. One thing I truly admire about my mother is her adherence to good manners. They stand her in good stead on this occasion; in fact, they are all that stop her from collapsing before we reach my flat. I quickly show her the workings of the place and then disappear to the baby clinic, telling her I'll be back at midday.

Mum has regained some of her equilibrium and is happily cleaning my flat when I return. I knew I shouldn't have bothered beforehand. She has discovered four packets of oral contraceptives in a drawer and subtly asks about them. I explain that contraception is frowned upon by the sisters so any of the Aboriginal women here that ask for the pill receive it from me, via the doctor. The rights and wrongs of Catholic ethics come a poor second to freedom of choice in my book. Maria joins us for lunch and we both try to emphasise the positive aspects of Port Keats and the people here, while acknowledging the numerous problems. We take Mum on a tour of the place and she finds it just as depressing as I first did.

Maria and I organise a card game for the evening with our neighbours, Leo, Cecily and Father Brendan. Leo and Cecily are veterans of the Papua New Guinea lay missionary experience and are less than thrilled with life in Port Keats. They hanker for the days of rigid certainty and the authoritarian rule of the Church. They have been here twelve months and are anxious to move. Father Brendan is eighteen months into his posting and has the job of facilitating the change from a paternalistic missionary church to one of self-determination and cultural inclusiveness. I'm not sure how he feels about his role here; the transfer of power is never easy and the inevitability of change often sweeps personal preferences aside.

The evening is going really well until the police arrive and inform Leo and Cecily that their house has been broken into. We all traipse across to investigate and poor Cecily is distraught when she sees and smells the faeces that has been smeared around. Immediately taking charge, my mother volunteers Maria and me to clean up the house while she shepherds Leo and Cecily back to my flat. God, I love mothers! Maria and I clean up the mess and discover several petrol containers that the kids must have used for sniffing. Petrol sniffing is a big problem in some Aboriginal communities and is just starting to get a grip here. By the time we return to my flat, Mum has heard every negative story relating to Port Keats and the Aboriginal race in general. This holiday is off to a great start.

Over the coming days I try to give my mother a positive view of my life up here. She is a big hit in the baby clinic and all the Aboriginal people are fascinated to meet her. Family is intrinsic to the Aboriginal way of life and I think they sometimes wonder about we whitefellas and our solitary state. The most frequent question my mother is asked is, 'What colour Tracey's father?' My mother's skin is very pale and my olive complexion only needs to know that the sun is shining to turn a deep shade of brown. There is much disbelief when my mother claims my father as white. Maria, several of the health workers and I take Mum out fishing one evening and slowly but surely she starts to adapt to the way of life here.

We even provide the dramatic entertainment of a premature birth. Maria is on call when one of the women goes into labour one evening. She is only thirty-seven weeks pregnant. We set her up in our own labour ward and try to radio through to a doctor in Darwin to have the medical plane come out and collect her. The radio is a wonderful connection to the outside world but rarely works once the sun goes down. There are all sorts of scientific reasons for this defect but they are never comforting when we have an emergency. All the pregnant women of Port Keats routinely go to Darwin in their thirty-eighth week and stay there until delivery. It is a terrible wrench for them but the practice has been instigated to cater for the unusual rather than the normal delivery. I know that Maria and I would be much happier if this woman were in Darwin right now.

My mother worked in a maternity hospital for many years and finds the whole situation quite entertaining. In her midwifery days the majority of deliveries were attended to by the nurses, without much reliance on doctors. We have the girl's mother and another relative in attendance and once the delivery is under way we have two languages and several voices all giving directions at the same time.

The labour only lasts a couple of hours before Maria delivers a small female child and then passes her to me. Fortunately a little oxygen and stimulation elicit a reasonable cry and, after I have performed all the ritual newborn tests and given her an injection, I hand her over to the grandmother. After delivery, the room is inundated with all the members of the extended family so Maria, Mum and I retire for a cup of tea and cigarettes. We thank our lucky stars that everything turned out smoothly.

The next unscheduled experience for my mother is a funeral. One of the old men has died and, as this was not unexpected, we hold the funeral as soon as the relatives wish. We have a proper single-body morgue refrigerator and the body is contained in an official plastic body-bag that we obtain from the police. The funeral service is, of course, Catholic. The body is placed on a stretcher loaded onto the tray back of the priest's truck and driven to the church. I am accompanying the body and, as we turn rather sharply towards the church, the stretcher starts to slide off the back of the truck. I fling myself across the body and manage to pull it back to its previous position, hoping that nobody has noticed my performance.

Once inside the church I sit with my mother and Maria and the service gets under way. The inside of the Port Keats church is decorated by Aboriginal artists and the altar and lectern are made from whole trees. A very large, black Jesus and a variety of animals provide the backdrop to the altar. It is the most beautiful and moving church that I've ever attended.

Everything is going along normally until my mother can stand it no longer and whispers, rather loudly, that the least the priest could have done was find out the old man's name. Throughout the service Father Brendan has referred to the deceased as 'this old man'. We inform Mum that it is against Aboriginal custom to refer by name to someone that has died. This explanation only partly satisfies my mother, who is a past master at critiquing priests' homilies.

I'm afraid Brendan has scored very poorly on this occasion.

The last but by no means least of my mother's impromptu holiday experiences is a wedding. I had no idea this was taking place until today. Together with virtually all the inhabitants of Port Keats we file into church for this surreal occasion. Ten couples are getting married and the whole set-up reminds me of the Moonies. The girls are seated on one side of the church, the guys on the other. Each couple rises in turn and moves forward together to recite their vows. They are so painfully shy that I have no idea what they are saying. Each time the priest asks a couple if they will have children as part of the marriage, we all start to giggle. One of the teachers who has been here for a few years gives us a running commentary on how long each couple has been together and how many children they already have. The church hasn't completely lost its grip here but slowly the numbers are dwindling.

My mother has now completed the trifecta of births, deaths and marriages!

 A few weeks after my mother's visit we hold the Port Keats baby show. When the health workers and Maria first told me about this annual event I couldn't believe they were serious. It is not your usual type of baby show and the enthusiasm of the health workers eventually wore me down. This is obviously a big event for the community and the many extra hours needed to organise it will hopefully be worthwhile. First the health workers wrote letters to all the big baby product companies, telling them about our baby show and asking for their support. The only one to come on board was Johnson & Johnson, who sent a box of their product samples. We received a large number of clothes from Catholic Missions in Darwin and most of the white residents hit on their relatives down south to provide prizes. The biggest contributors were John and Carol, the store managers, who filled any gaps in our prize lists.

To say that this is a baby show with a difference is probably an understatement. The competition categories include: 'best weight gain', 'best skin' and 'most improved health performance'. The entire under-five population is taken into account and many different age categories are formed. It is my job to wade through every single chart to find our best performers. This is an exhausting and time-consuming occupation and the further I delve into the charts the more mothers and children I find whose efforts really should be acknowledged. As a result, many categories are what I call 'seasonally adjusted and expanded'.

Everybody in the community is involved to some extent. Even at the club I'm continually being stopped by different men who spend precious drinking time waxing lyrical about the attributes of their particular children. Occasionally I'm offered cans of beer for my trouble. Unfortunately I have to protect the integrity of the umpire and decline. It is wonderful to see all these very macho men taking such an interest in a baby show.

When my mother was here, parents would stop by the flat to canvass her opinion on various hairstyles and dresses that the babies and children were to wear. I keep telling everyone that it is a health show and I shall judge purely from the records, but enthusiasm is building inexorably and a baby show here turns out to be no different emotionally from anywhere else on the planet. Apparently we are to have judges of a sort who will choose a child from each section for a special prize. No person in their right mind would volunteer for this job so we have to go outside the community to recruit some fearless people. We convince Sister Yvonne to come over from Daly River for the occasion and, as luck will have it, Maria has a sister coming for a holiday just at the opportune time. My mother doesn't know how lucky she is to be safely home in Toowoomba.

As the time draws close, the mechanics of staging this event occupy most of my thinking. Past baby shows have been held on the verandah of the main clinic and, as the show is supposed to start at 10.00 a.m., it will be fiercely hot. When I suggest we use the club instead, I'm met with horrified faces. According to the women it is a men's only area and the men would never let us use it. Games of pool was the club's only daytime activity. I have spent a lot of my time here trying to encourage the women to stand up for their rights without much success. If I can get the men to give us the club for the morning, I ask them, will all the women come? Hardly any of the women in Port Keats and certainly none of the children have ever been inside the club since it was built. They tell me they are happy to use it but are sure that I'll never get the men's agreement. My insider knowledge of the men's passionate interest in the baby show is something that I keep to myself. I approach the club manager with my request and after he has discussed it with a few of the men he agrees to let us use the place.

Preparation for the big day is running at fever pitch. The health workers and mothers in the baby clinic spend all day making decorations and posters. As with any small community, eventually everyone becomes involved. The blatant attempts to interfere with my judicial impartiality are reaching epidemic proportions. Now members of the white community are pushing the merits of their particular favourites.

There seems to be an informal, unspoken system here where white people befriend their Aboriginal co-workers, thus extending the family unit. It is a great system and the only way for the two races to learn anything about each other. The whitefellas provide the transport to go bush and the blackfellas provide the knowledge to ensure that everybody has a safe and successful day's hunting, fishing or just communing with nature.

Finally the big day arrives and at ten o'clock the entire town shuts down. The school children and all the teachers arrive at the club. The store, council office, bank and post office are closed. This is better than Indira Gandhi's mourning period. The club is bedecked with streamers and balloons and the names of all the children are on posters around the walls. The plane carrying Sister Yvonne is late and we can't start without her. With the temperature in the mid-thirties and the humidity way over 100 per cent, the crush of bodies creates a sauna effect. There are hundreds of women and children in the club and quite a lot of men outside, trying to act very nonchalant. The noise level is deafening and I breathe a sigh of relief when I hear the plane swoop overhead.

We begin proceedings with the zero to six months age group. These are my particular favourites as a diet of breast milk provides all they need to reach that chubby baby stage. The judging and prize-giving goes along smoothly and John and Carol have supplied enough fruit to ensure that nobody leaves empty-handed. The entire baby show—this event for which we have been frenziedly preparing for weeks—is

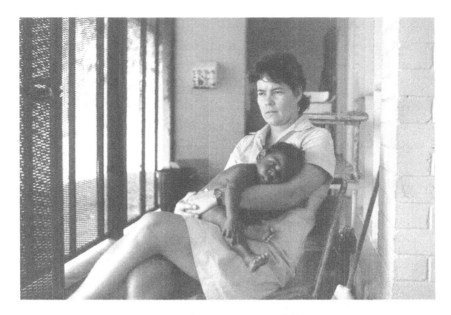

A reflective moment at the clinic

completed in just over an hour. When the clapping and cheering sounds have finally left my throbbing head, I'm greeted by a sight that reminds me of the post-Kalighat picnic scene. Once again I ask myself, is it all worth the effort?

I am drenched in sweat and the entire proceedings seem to have passed in a blur. I hate having to stand up and speak in public but I had been conned into running the whole show with a microphone. My stomach has completely shut down and I couldn't even draw on a calming cigarette to relieve my overloaded nervous system. Maria informs me that it was all a huge success, not even one disgruntled participant! I bet that's a first for a baby show. Eventually I regain

From beautiful babies to beautiful children

my equilibrium and snippets of the morning return to me. Naturally I am a biased observer but I do think that some of our babies would wipe the floor with any competition in the country.

The concept of a health baby show and the overwhelming community support has inspired a couple of teachers to write an article for a magazine. We are continually bombarded with negative stories about Aboriginal people and this seems like a good way to redress the balance. We meet in my flat—Mary, Leanne and Louise from the school; Maria, me, Agnes and Lillian from the clinic. Mary and Leanne outline their idea for the article; Louise, Agnes and Lillian give the Aboriginal perspective; while Maria and I outline the health benefits. Several hours later we come up with what I consider a terrific article. It has it all: tension, excitement, humour, colour, drama and a message. We even have colour slides to use in conjunction with the article. We send it off to the *Women's Weekly* and wait in anticipation for it to appear in print. The word about the article has spread around the town like wildfire and everyone wants to order a copy. We receive a reply several weeks later, thanking us for the article but explaining that they have already had an Aboriginal story for that month—all about a white physiotherapist working in outback Australia!

 I have been here long enough now to feel like I am part of the place. I can recognise and name nearly every child in my care. I have even reached the stage of being able to understand some of the Murringhpatha language. I practise every day in the baby clinic over morning tea. As we are centrally placed in Port Keats, most people have to pass by us to reach the store and other facilities, which leads to a lot of women stopping by to rest on their travels. Whenever two or more human beings are gathered together there will always be gossip exchanged. If I listen very carefully and decipher the people's Aboriginal names correctly, I can find out who's doing what to whom. I laughed after hearing about one illicit affair and the women nearly died of fright. I wasn't meant to understand. Eventually the culture and mannerisms become a part of me and I find myself giving directions with my lips and actually understanding what they mean. Even my thongs are discarded in favour of bare feet.

This can be a wonderful place to live and these are some of the nicest people I've ever met. But bubbling along below the surface are enormous frustrations for both races in the community. On the whole the resident white people work very hard in their particular fields, not only to do the best job they can but also to teach the Aborigines those same skills. The teaching is the easy part, as most Aboriginal workers are keen to learn. The frustrating part is that none of us can ever seem to show the statistical results which would prove that we are actually making a difference. Consequently people blame each other and the whitefella eventually leaves, usually after one or two years, passing the buck to the next person. The blackfellas get frustrated because in a town of 1300 there are only 100 jobs to go around. Everyone else is reliant on the government for their very survival and this breeds its own brand of resentment.

There is very little friction between the races, and both the black and white communities do everything they can to educate any new arrivals about the local customs. If we whitefellas wish to go out bush for any reason, we must first ask the permission of the traditional owners. This is a very simple courtesy and prevents us from being in sacred or forbidden areas during ceremonies. As this is still a very traditional community, a lot of ceremonies take place at different times during the year. It would create enormous problems if the whitefellas stumbled upon special ceremonies and disturbed the spirits. There is usually no difficulty in obtaining permission to visit anybody's land and in most cases some sound advice accompanies this assent. The same system operates for the different tribes living here as well.

The majority of conflicts arising in Port Keats stem from inter-tribal disputes. Ever since this community was established there have been troubles between the seven tribes. Grouping all these people together has made servicing and organising the community easier, but culturally it has produced decades of disputes and many tribal laws broken. Abuse of alcohol has only exacerbated the tensions that pervade the community.

It is into this amazing history of inter-tribal conflicts that I am drawn one evening. Maria has already left Port Keats and now works for the Air Medical Service in Darwin. Collette is a young nurse from Sydney who has joined us to do six months lay-missionary work. She calls me over to the clinic one evening to ask my opinion about a young girl. This girl has a roaring temperature, marked dehydration and is passing blood in her urine. She is only twelve years old and scared to death. Her relatives brought her in but have now mysteriously disappeared. I find this most remarkable and unusual in families here. I set up an intravenous and try to get some fluids into her, leaving Collette to try to bring the temperature down. My anger at the family for leaving this little girl alone is building and I storm out of the clinic and into a little white clinic truck to go and confront them. Awareness of my surroundings when I am in this particular frame of mind is not often what it should be, and as I drive up the main street I vaguely register the fact that a few hundred highly excited men are gathered into a crowd. I manoeuvre my vehicle around them, obliged to hastily wind up the windows as a flurry of spears descends on my little truck. Once around this obstacle I make my way to the house in question and jump out, demanding that someone return to the clinic with me. The church is very close to this house and I can see all manner of disturbance occurring there, but I will not be deterred from my quest and eventually the grandmother gets in the truck and accompanies me back to the clinic. I take another route back but the whole town seems to be caught up in some form of madness. Once I have the grandmother sitting with the girl, Collette and I start trying to contact a doctor in Darwin. The radio, as usual, is on the blink now that the sun has gone down.

The clinic is soon deluged with victims from the night's fighting and as the numbers grow I make sure the clinic's defences are maintained. All the doors are made of metal and these are locked; all the windows are unbreakable plastic. We institute a policy of only letting in casualties, who are to be treated and released as quickly as possible. The majority of the injuries are superficial and require suturing and dressings. I have become something of an expert in the art of sewing since arriving in Port Keats and most of the health workers are capable in this area as well. I try to move the patients on as quickly as possible so that the clinic does not become a focus for the fighting. The entire population seems to be involved in this conflict.

Our problems get even worse when the police arrive, bringing a wounded man with them. He has been stabbed several times and has a few deep head lacerations as well. According to the police the town is in a riot and, as they have no control over it, they will stay here and try to contact Darwin via the radio. As luck will have it, the man who has been stabbed is

the father of the little girl in the next room. I also
know him well from the number of times I have had
to stitch up his wife after he has come home drunk.
A further investigation of this man's injuries reveals
tell-tale frothing from the wound on the back of his
right shoulder. He has a punctured lung. While this
is a serious problem I am able to seal the wound and
prevent any further deflation of the lung. He has also
been drinking heavily and is in a pretty mellow mood
considering the night's activities. I have very little sympathy for him and I inform him that I'm more worried
about his daughter's condition than his. I also consider it poetic justice that he now needs sewing up
after the number of times I've had to treat his wife.
She has joined the other women around her daughter's bed. By the time I finish dealing with his injuries,
he has promised me a hundred times that he will turn
over a new leaf, give up the grog and become a good
husband and father. I wish I had a dollar for every
time I've heard that refrain in this clinic. Anyway, he
is resting comfortably with an oxygen mask in place
and that's about all I can do for him now.

There is a large gathering of very angry people outside the clinic and some of them are wailing as if
somebody has died. I quickly realise that they are all
family members of this man and have assumed the
worst. It's true that he didn't look all that flash when
they carried him in covered with blood. I unlock the
door and yell on top note that he is okay and not
going to die. My still-bubbling anger spurs me on to
tell them that if they want to pray for anybody it
should be the little girl because she is much sicker

than her father. This news has the desired effect of subduing the crowd and eventually everyone returns to their homes. I have no idea what is happening in the rest of the town but for the first time tonight the clinic is calm.

Our main problem is the useless radio. The police have contacted everyone in town with radios and requested them to keep trying to reach Darwin. Eventually Brother Vince comes over to tell us that he has been able to make contact with somebody in Perth via his CB radio. This man will contact the Darwin police and medical authorities for us. We light the kerosene lamps on the airstrip and wait, praying for a speedy answer to our call for help. Around three in the morning, two planes land, one containing six police reinforcements and the other the usual medical plane with two doctors. It is something of an anti-climax to drive through a quiet and peaceful town. At the clinic I send one doctor to look at the little girl and another to assess the father. They must insert a chest tube before he can be taken on the plane, and the doctor makes me assist so that I can learn how to do it for future emergencies. I can live without learning some things! Eventually our patients are ready for evacuation, and as the town is once again calm both doctors decide to return to Darwin.

This whole night sticks in my mind because the diagnosis of the little girl turns out to be measles, and during the following weeks we have dozens of babies and children falling prey to this illness. I have never seen such severe reactions and we have to keep the children here to stop it spreading to other settlements.

The entire staff and relatives nurse these children around the clock and only when the complications become too severe do we send them to hospital in Darwin. Even with a near 100 per cent immunisation record these kids still contract measles. The last straw for me is when two babies, both too young to be immunised, die as a result of complications. I've read about the effect of Western diseases on the Aboriginal population during the early years but to actually see the devastation in action is a horrifying sight.

There has been more pain, suffering and loss during this outbreak than ever occurred with the spears and bullets on the night of the riot. I still have no idea what caused it. All I ever heard were mumblings of 'bad business'. It certainly made for a very subdued community for many months to come. The Darwin newspaper ran a feature on the riot, but unfortunately the death of children by measles didn't rate a mention. Stereotypes obviously make much more palatable reading.

 As the months turn into years I find myself part and parcel of the fabric of Port Keats. I've learnt much from the Aborigines and the whitefellas here and also discovered many facets of bureaucracies. Each has contributed in their own way to making the challenge of surviving in a place like this both a golden dream and your worst nightmare.

With the Aborigines I have learnt the crafts of bush survival and can now find food and water in the most mundane and apparently barren landscape. As with all things in my life thus far, this knowledge has been gained during many hilarious and often disastrous expeditions with my black and white friends. I've eaten all manner of flora and fauna and have generally lived by the principle of trying anything once. I have eaten sea turtles and turtle eggs and am now happy in the knowledge that I'll never have to eat another. The all-time worst experience for my tastebuds has been the ingestion of a mangrove worm. This fat, slimy, white delicacy lives in rotting mangrove trees and is pounced upon with absolute relish by the Aboriginal population. My particular brush with this gourmet's delight was when Lillian handed me a

30-centimetre specimen straight from the tree and I foolishly opened my mouth and let it slide in. The taste of mud and slime will stay with me forever. I can, however, recommend fruit bats. All that self-marinating on mangoes lends a lovely flavour to the flesh.

Port Keats is the only place I've been to in Australia where if we see a kangaroo on the road we try to run it over. This particular practice has seen us come closer to killing ourselves than the wildlife. I have also participated in the world-wide practice of shooting and butchering cattle. This lot are better equipped in the limb department than the lepers of Pulambaddy, but everything else is just as basic.

Every July nearly the entire local population of Port Keats goes bush. All the different family groups go out to their own country for the entire month. Many members of the white community use their vehicles to transport these groups. The only things they take with them are some foam mattresses, blankets, flour, tea, sugar and a billy can. In one instance this particular custom helped save the children from another viral outbreak. I discovered a child just returned from Darwin with chicken pox, so before she had contact with other children, I persuaded her entire family to go bush for a couple of weeks, accompanied by one of the health workers who happened to be a relation. It brings a whole new meaning to the term isolation ward! This entire month of July is like a form of cleansing, though the lure of the club proves too great for some of the men.

I now know that when the Aborigines look at their land and sea their view is different from mine. For them it is a supermarket, a hardware store, a pharmacy, a library, a museum, a place of worship, an art gallery, and all of these things interconnect within their souls. They have shown me all these different aspects but I can only ever see one at a time. I doubt whether anybody not born into this culture can ever fully understand the true meaning of 'country'. What really frustrates me is watching the steady erosion of an ancient lifestyle by Western civilisation. Like many whitefellas I would love to build a bubble around these people and only let in the positive aspects of Western life. But I recognise that this is a form of paternalism and, hard as it may seem, these people

Jonathan and Annunciata, Port Keats

have the right to make their own mistakes. God only knows we've made enough of our own.

The white community here has proven to be fairly similar to the volunteer community in Calcutta. Whenever people are markedly in the minority, they tend to band together for support. We have had the most outlandish parties known to man and everyone, including the priest and nuns, has been invited. These parties usually have a theme and some of the highlights have been the mock wedding, the 'P' (dress as something beginning with the letter P) party, the accident and emergency party, the Queensland party and the toga party. Our all-time ultimate social occasion was for the 'Person Port Keats Quest'. This particular evening surpassed all others in demonstrating the lengths some people will go to in order to amuse themselves. As well as the parties, there are the more traditional activities—cards, fishing and barbecues. Our lives are full and exciting and we very rarely feel the need to go to Darwin and experience civilisation. When we do go to town we tend to be very protective of Port Keats and its reputation. More than one fight has been started over the various merits of different Aboriginal settlements.

Racism is something that is a part of life. It affects each person differently and each person expresses it differently. As whitefellas, we very rarely feel the negative impact of personal racism because of the colour of our skin. But when I have been to Darwin with Agnes or Lillian and witnessed the blatant discrimination they are subjected to, my blood starts to boil and they have to restrain my anger. If I were a blackfella,

I think I'd be a terrorist. I must also admit that there is racism among the Aboriginal population. Just goes to prove we are all the same under the skin.

The truly hard part of living in a place like Port Keats is the frustration. Everything we try to achieve in the clinic just seems to get us nowhere. I have tried to emphasise the importance of good nutrition, but am between a rock and a hard place. The shop here sells mainly canned goods and the fresh produce they do supply is so expensive most people cannot afford to buy it. Fresh fruit is a luxury and we receive only powdered milk. The one bonus is the local bakery which produces bread five days a week. We have a takeaway shop which sells cooked chickens, hot chips and pies. It seems futile to preach about good nutrition when most people cannot access the recommended food. The other major obstacle to better nutrition is the squandering of money. Each fortnight thousands of dollars pour into Port Keats in the form of social security cheques. The speed with which this money evaporates is truly amazing. Everyone buys up big at the store and then it is time to sit down and play cards in the hope of winning 'big' money. After two days most of the money has disappeared and people live hand-to-mouth for the next twelve days. There is always the bush and the sea to sustain people, but the life of a hunter–gatherer requires enormous effort and patience compared to the ease of a store.

Most whitefellas here tend to last about two years. I have been here for two and a half, and can feel my enthusiasm draining away. The never-ending frustration with the lack of any substantive change in the children's health and the physical tiredness that constant on-call work involves combine to produce a form of apathy. The people here deserve better and in October of 1987 I resign my post and decide to have a well-earned break. It is rather a drastic step but the only way I can see out of this malaise.

The most painful aspect of this departure is that I have finally found a man here. Glen is employed as a mechanic and is also a wonderful cook, which has further raised his prospects in my estimation. This relationship has survived the last few turbulent months and I can only hope that once I have my body and soul back in sync, we may get back together.

FORTY-THREE

 When in doubt, return to the familiar. I am back in Calcutta again. I flew here straight from Darwin and this time it is a completely different experience. Now I am not poor and can afford a twin-bed room in the Modern Lodge all to myself. I have a visa for three months and this time have no intention of extending. I need to revitalise myself, to find the fun in life. Calcutta strips life to its basics and provides me with a blueprint for what is really necessary. The seemingly insurmountable problems of Port Keats have left me burnt out.

Calcutta is the same as ever and the day after I arrive I bump into an old friend. Ajit calmly says, 'I expected you last weekend.' This amazes me as I hadn't told him I was returning, but then he tells me that two days ago in Calcutta Australia won the World Cup in cricket and he had a feeling that I would be here. Ajit and I have known each other since 1981 and we immediately sit down and discuss all that has occurred in the last few years. This city of millions seems sometimes as small as the settlement of Port Keats.

My return to Kalighat inspires Sister Luke to take me on yet another tour of all the improvements that have occurred in my absence. The most remarkable transformation has been the removal from the roof of the Indian workers, who have been replaced by the sisters. I have always thought that the sisters should have a 24-hour presence here and I'm pleased that it has finally happened. Sister Luke and three other sisters live in specially built rooftop rooms, while the former residents have been firmly established in a village outside Calcutta. The drama involved in this move takes Sister Luke many hours to cover fully. I'm relieved to have missed that particular period. I am more than happy just to quietly feed and clean the patients and leave all the medical/nursing procedures to those volunteers already doing such work. They can have all the headaches, I am here for a holiday.

I am twenty-seven years of age now and feel about ninety-seven. I'm an elder statesman in the volunteer community, although not the sisters' idea of an ideal volunteer. Sister Luke points me in the direction of another like-minded soul, an Englishman named Simon who has also been to Kalighat on a previous trip. We help each other lighten the mood and inject a little fun back into the place. It is through Simon that I meet two New Zealand nurses and discover that they are working with Dr Jack.

Dr Jack Praeger has lived in Calcutta for many years and I first met him when we were both residents of the YWCA in 1981. In those days he worked on his own and was just starting to organise his operation on a bigger scale. Today he has an organisation called

Calcutta Rescue which holds street clinics and runs feeding programs. Jack runs his clinic on the footpath opposite the Y, much to the horror of the residents in Middleton Row. Pandering to the sensibilities of the more affluent has never been his long suit and he has had a running battle with the governmental authorities for years. His aim is to employ local Indian workers wherever possible, and he is also attracting his fair share of volunteers. The sisters can't stand him or his attitudes and have somewhat demonised the man, but there are enough poor people in Calcutta to accommodate more than one outlook on life. I spend a few mornings helping in his clinic and in the afternoons I sing his praises to Sister Luke. This leads her to deliver a stark sermon on the many heresies that Jack is supposed to have uttered.

I walk into Kalighat one afternoon and, as I'm hanging up my bag, Sister Luke informs me that we have someone famous working here. Apparently there is a rumour that a prominent American politician is among the ranks of the volunteers. Famous visitors are nothing new to Kalighat and Sister Luke's dearest dream is that one day we shall be graced by a visit from the Pope. We have had cardinals, royalty, politicians and sports people pass through these walls on their tours of Calcutta. Perhaps cynically, I see us located somewhere between the zoo and the museum on tourist brochures.

Volunteers come in all shapes and sizes, and as Sister Luke and I survey the male volunteers we narrow the possibilities of our celebrity down to two men. Sister Luke loves the idea of somebody famous actually working here in Kalighat. Simon and I make some investigations and decide that the older, more distinguished-looking volunteer named Jerry is our secret star. We learn that his last name is Brown, but as we know nothing about American politics this means nothing to us. Eventually I just ask him and he tells us that he was Governor of California a few years ago. This news makes no difference to any of the volunteers but pleases Sister Luke no end. I also elicit the more important information that Jerry is staying at the Fairlawn Hotel and, as such, has a bathtub and hot water at his disposal. A quiet reminder about the Christian values of sharing has Jerry offering me the use of his tub at my earliest convenience.

The leaked news of this famous person's presence in Calcutta soon produces an avalanche of requests from government and non-government organisations for Jerry to go and inspect their work. I'm not sure what any of this is supposed to accomplish, but thank my lucky stars that I'm not famous. Jerry spends about three weeks in Calcutta, working just like any other volunteer, and then he is gone.

My other exciting brush with fame comes when I get to meet members of the Bolshoi Ballet at the Pink Elephant nightclub in the Grand Hotel. I can now honestly say that I've danced with the Bolshoi! God, I love Calcutta.

I spend another Christmas here and am slowly but surely rediscovering the simple things in life. I have brought an album of Port Keats photographs with me and have shown them to all the sisters, volunteers, workers and patients. I feel a need to go back and find my niche. Sister Luke still holds out hope that I'll join the blue-bordered brigade but that is far from my thoughts. My three months here has brought me back to life and I now feel ready to return to the Northern Territory and resume my life.

The absurdity of Calcutta and Kalighat being a source of rejuvenation is not lost on me, but then I've always had doubts about my mental condition.

 I return to Port Keats in January and move in with Glen, who has fortunately stayed in touch while I have been sorting out my life. Not that I have any idea what I will now do except live here and see if we can survive together. At least I'm calmer than when I left and unlikely to inflict unpremeditated violence on the community at large. There is no work for me in the clinic so Liam and Maureen offer me a temporary job in the takeaway. The mere thought of working around food is enough to reduce me to fits of laughter. I am well aware that my one and only culinary triumph in Calcutta all those years ago does not qualify me as any kind of chef.

I work from 7.00 a.m. till midday, and before long I've mastered the art of cooking chickens on the rotisserie, frying chips, and making hot dogs and salad rolls. After several near-fatal attempts I have even conquered the curried chicken and rice. The people of Port Keats find my new career move just as baffling as does my family. I dispense nutritional advice and judiciously change orders as I'm selling the food, trying to convince myself that I'm doing my part to improve the health of the community. It is a great way to see another side of life in this town and it's basically stress-free. I spend my afternoons going bush with Lillian, Agnes and some of the women that work in the take-away. This lifestyle is very seductive and I wonder if I'll ever want to change again.

As part of my work in the takeaway, I prepare the meals for the pensioners. We have a meals-on-wheels scheme which drives around picking up the pension-ers and depositing them near the main clinic. The driver then comes and collects the chicken and veg-etable stew that I have made and delivers it to the pensioners. I have tried to add a little variety to this daily meal, but each time I exercise my imagination the verdict is depressingly negative. If I can't even impress this group with my culinary prowess I fear my days in the catering field are numbered.

To my own amazement, I survive four months in the takeaway. At this point Maureen and I discuss my unsuitability to the food environment and I realise I'll never be really happy until I'm back nursing. And I know I have to strike while the iron is hot. A phone call offering my services to the rural health depart-ment in Darwin surprisingly produces an instant job offer, this time as a rural relief nurse anywhere in the top third of the Northern Territory. I now have to return to the flat and tell Glen of my momentous decision. He is happy with my choice and we will try to organise our weekends together when I start in Adelaide River in a month's time. We both value our independence too much to worry about the future.

*

I start my new life with a week in a health clinic in Palmerston, just outside of Darwin. This is the closest I've been to working in civilisation for many years and it takes a little getting used to. I had almost finished sewing up a laceration on a man's foot when I realised that I was supposed to send him to a doctor. The patient promised not to say anything as long as I finished the job. Fortunately I only have to survive one week here, and at least it gives me an opportunity to acclimatise myself to the Department of Health's way of doing things. God, I just love learning about new paperwork.

My next destination is an Aboriginal settlement in Arnhem Land called Oenpelli. I have a three-week relieving job here. This is different country from Port Keats, situated, as it is, just on the edge of Kakadu National Park. The people are a different tribe and speak a completely different language. One drawback to these short relieving jobs is that there isn't time to learn how to pronounce people's names. The surname is the Aboriginal family name and the people of Oenpelli seem to have particularly long names. As always, it is the Aboriginal health workers who provide much of the information needed in order that poor, stupid whitefellas may function competently. The social and health problems here are the same as at Port Keats, except that they have more liberal alcohol laws here and consequently drink is a bigger problem. Unlike Port Keats there seem to be few inter-tribal conflicts in Oenpelli. I am just starting to feel comfortable here when my time is up and then I'm off to Adelaide River.

I have a three-month engagement at Adelaide River, and I will be on my own. The only accommodation available is a bed in the clinic itself, and as I'm on call twenty-four hours a day this seems appropriate. It is certainly more comfortable and cleaner than some places I've stayed in during these last few years.

Adelaide River is a small, white and Aboriginal community about one hour south of Darwin. My main task is to keep the clinic functioning and to make visits to a couple of goldmines and one of the bigger stations. There is not a great deal of work to do—some days I'm lucky to get one customer. I can generally amuse myself anywhere and the time passes faster than I could have imagined.

*

It is near the end of my time in Adelaide River that I drive over to Port Keats for the weekend. I take Margaret, the wife of the plumber, and her three children with me as her car won't be able to cope with the dirt roads. We have a wonderful weekend and are just outside Adelaide River on our return journey when the engine gives a cough and dies. Fortunately two vehicles come along shortly after we stop and they offer to give us a tow into town.

We are all hooked up and on our way, but before I realise what's happening I find myself driving over the tow rope with my car veering off to the left. I grip the steering wheel to cushion the impact of a small tree looming in front of me and the next thing I know, the entire car has rolled over, leaving me unsure whether I'm up or down. I cannot move a muscle and feel as if the entire roof of the car is pressing down on my head. My mouth and brain still work, though, and once I have ascertained the children are fine and Margaret is not badly hurt, I feel a great sense of relief. Our good Samaritans are in a great state of anxiety; one of them leans down to tell me that they'll go to Adelaide River and get the nurse. 'I am the fucking nurse,' I reply, and direct him to the house to which the regular nurse has just returned.

Many hours later and with police, ambulance and the nurse in attendance, I am freed from my metal entanglements. All I can feel is the most excruciating pain in my neck. They lay me on the ground, apply a neck brace, and then transfer me to a stretcher in the ambulance. One look at the worried faces of the people around me is enough to send my spirits plummeting. I have been conscious throughout this ordeal and my brain knows that I can't feel anything below my shoulders, but the rest of my body is resisting this information.

The trip to Darwin is agonisingly slow as the ambulance crew keep stopping every twenty minutes to check my vital signs. I threaten death if they stop the vehicle once more, as the pain in my neck with every stop and start movement is unbearable. My other great concern is a stabbing pain at the back of my head and a very real sensation that ants are biting my scalp. It takes a little time to convince the ambulance attendant that I'm not suffering from head injuries and am completely serious in my complaint. Determined to shut me up, she starts combing through my hair where, much to her surprise, she discovers several large green ants. The reason for the pain in the back of my head turns out to be a sharp piece of twig. We hasten to Darwin without further incident, and I lie back on the stretcher and hope that this is all some horrible nightmare.

In Darwin, X-rays conclude that I have dislocated the 5th cervical vertebrae and fractured the 6th and 7th vertebrae. This is as bad as it gets. I have the staff contact a friend of mine in Darwin to whom I entrust the job of ringing my mother and breaking the news. I am now a quadriplegic and I don't know if I'll ever be able to accept it.

 Four days after the accident I'm transferred to the Spinal Injuries Unit at the Princess Alexandra Hospital in Brisbane. This is where reality really kicks in. I now have two metal tongs drilled into my skull and these are joined, by a U-shaped piece of metal, to a rope and pulley attached to the head of the bed. The rope extends down to a bag of weights which acts as traction against my broken bones. My neck is four times its normal size and looks like something out of a horror movie. Apart from this, all I have to show for the extent of damage to my body is a minuscule graze on my head.

The doctors here are specialists in spinal injuries and they have the standard talk down pat. I have a complete spinal cord injury at level C 6/7 and as a result have lost all feeling and movement from the chest down, including bladder and bowel. I have lost feeling and movement in some of my arm muscles and completely in my hands. The only bright note in this litany of woe is that if any nerves do recover it usually happens in the first few months post-injury; however, they are not that hopeful in my case. I don't like being on this side of the bed at all.

My treatment consists of thirteen weeks in traction. Life as I knew it ceased to exist on 23 October 1988. Strangely enough, that line in the tourist brochure about Calcutta assaulting the senses is uppermost in my mind now. The senses are all I have left and if Calcutta was an assault, this is all-out bloody war.

Life attached to a bed doesn't offer much in the way of excitement for the sense of sight. I am in a mechanical bed and am turned from the left side to my back and then to my right side every four hours. These are my three views of life. The left-hand view faces the corridor and nurses' station and I find this side very tiring and frustrating. To watch people scurrying around when you can barely move a muscle is exhausting. Watching the nurses perform duties that I had been doing only one week ago is pure torture. But probably the most upsetting image is that of all the other quadriplegics and paraplegics wheeling around in their chairs. I try to block all this out, and discover that with a little practice I can mind-travel back to Calcutta and Port Keats and all the places that I've been happy in during my life.

The ceiling is typical of most hospitals and comprises sections of little squares inside larger panels. There is the odd stain or two and I can while away many hours doing mathematical calculations and inventing stories about the figures I recognise in the stains. I come to the conclusion that no hospital should ever be built with pure white ceilings and I can envisage a whole new art-and-design field opening up in the decoration of ceilings.

The right-side view is my favourite. This faces a wall and glass doors that open out onto a view of gum trees, grass and the sky. Nature is just as wonderful wherever you are and it always gives me hope and a feeling of wellbeing.

My hearing has always been acute and it is even more so now. Sounds begin to bring very distinctive messages. I can tell the mood of a nurse by the way she walks into the room. I learn that their faces and mouths try to deceive but the good old feet never succumb to play-acting. Hospitals are extremely noisy places and how anyone believes you can rest in them is beyond me. It is a cacophony that includes mops and buckets, floor polishers, food trolleys, mobile medical aids, hundreds of feet, beds, wheelchairs, televisions and voices. As the weeks go by I learn to distinguish each and every sound, and then learn how to tune out. At night there is always some patient yelling out for a nurse. In a twisted piece of logic the nurses always remember to leave the call button on the bed and close to your body. This is fine for the paras but as useful as an ashtray on a motorcycle to us quads with our useless hands.

Another of the senses that is not a great bonus in hospital is the sense of taste. We have a two-week rotating menu and, much to my disgust, something called 'chopped chicken in gravy' appears in both weeks. The P. A. Hospital is surrounded by takeaway restaurants for a very good reason and every visitor I receive is quickly dispatched to find some form of appetising food. I have a whole new sympathy for the patients of Kalighat now that I am on the receiving end of many forks and spoons. There is an art to feeding someone flat on their back, or even on their side, and most people don't have it. Food loses a lot of its charm when you are spoon-fed and soon everything starts to taste like everything else.

Eating and drinking in bed when you are completely immobilised can be a life-threatening experience. The water jug and tubing may look benign but if the person with the jug holds it above the level of your head when you place the tube in your mouth and suck, an inevitable gravity effect comes into play and drowning becomes a very real possibility. I have discovered, however, that cans of rum and coke can be successfully imbibed through the tube— the more the merrier! (Beer never tastes the same when sipped through a straw.) My other necessity of life is, of course, a cigarette and it takes little to persuade the nurses to wheel my bed out onto the verandah and light up a smoke for both of us. Nurses always need a cigarette.

Smell is perhaps the sense most offended against in a hospital. The combination of disinfectant, floor polish, faeces, urine, dead flowers and perspiration make a heady mix at different times of the day. There is also the distinctive smell of different takeaway meals that visitors bring onto the ward every day. The pizza man even does deliveries to your bed.

Touch is both a curse and a beacon of hope. At least a hundred times a day I run a mental inventory of what I can feel and move. I concentrate my entire being and run a check on my body from my toes to my head. This process is an emotional roller-coaster of hope and devastation, but is like a drug that I can't live without. I can feel my head and shoulders, and this 10 per cent of my body screams for 100 per cent of my attention. A simple task such as blowing a blocked nose requires help from another person and never achieves a satisfactory result. An itchy scalp seems to be my constant companion and at times I feel like I'm lying on an ants' nest. My most dreaded experience is when a lone mosquito decides to call; that uniquely piercing scream reverberates in my head. On many occasions my arm has risen in a reflex motion to fight off my buzzing nemesis, only to come crashing down on my metal skull attachments, thus further enhancing the pain experience. I eventually learn, in some Pavlovian fashion, that some inconveniences are better left ignored.

The other significant facet of life attached to a bed is time. There is far too much time to think. The usual questions of 'Why?' and 'What if?' ... dominate my thinking. For some unknown reason I've been anointed three times since my accident. It is called 'the blessing of the sick'. It is not your final send-off, but a fairly normal response to catastrophe in Catholic circles. I have also had the dubious honour of hearing every religious cliche in the book regarding suffering and God's plan. This is another one of the consequences of immobility—the inability to escape unwanted visitors. It has amazed me how many people seem to be able to decipher the hand of God in illnesses and accidents. If I hear once more that God doesn't give you more than you can bear, I swear I'll throw up. It is interesting to observe that these people never seem to be chosen for the suffering themselves. One too many of these sanctimonious visitors strains my natural good manners to breaking point and my next visitor to mouth senseless crap is told to piss off.

I do believe in God, if not wholeheartedly in organised religions. I cannot believe in God playing some sort of game with people's lives. He is an easy figure to blame when things go wrong. I'm more of a fatalist and don't read any more into my present condition than pure bad luck. I spend hours reliving that evening, and by changing just the slightest piece in the picture my life continues as before. This is fruitless thinking, but I am unable to stop myself rewriting history every day. I think about all the people I have met and nursed over the years and the hundreds I have seen die. I do not fear death and in many ways would welcome it. Many times when I'm rewriting history I make sure that the accident is a fatal one. This is also fruitless thinking but comforting in its own strange way. The big surprise in my many thinking sessions is the number of people I wouldn't trade places with. I now have some appreciation for the physical deformity of the lepers, but even though many of them are mobile I couldn't bring myself to swap quadriplegia for leprosy. Another group that receives a negative response is the destitute of Calcutta. The mere fact of surviving is not life for me. The last group is the Aborigines. I don't think I could live in this society as a black person without committing violence against all the little discriminations, let alone the major ones. I'm much safer in a wheelchair, and so is the Aboriginal cause.

Unwittingly the prisoners of Boggo Road jail provide not only entertainment but inspiration for us inhabitants of the Spinal Unit. Whenever they stage a break-out we line the verandah and cheer them on. They have a better chance of escaping their bars than we do and, while they are not always successful, at least they have a go at escaping. This attitude opens a small window in my mind. Life will go on and maybe my adventures are not finished yet.

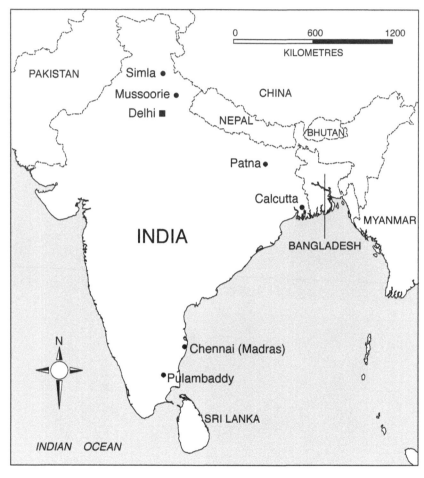

Map 1   India

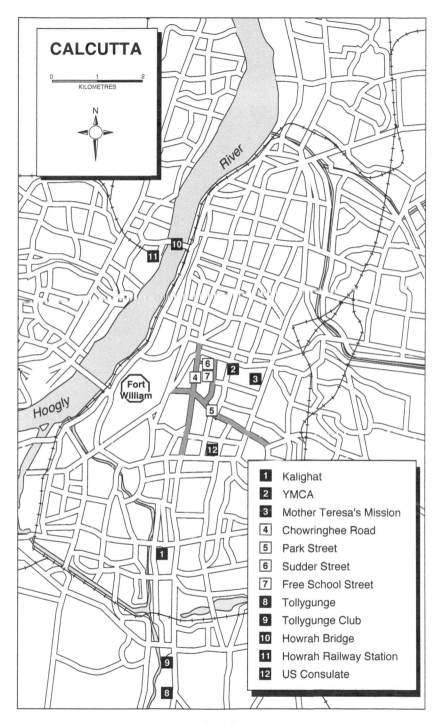

Map 2   Calcutta

Map 3   Northern Territory, Australia